THE ART OF GONE WITH THE WIND

◆ THE ART OF ◆
GONE WITH THE WIND
THE MAKING OF A LEGEND

Judy Cameron and Paul J. Christman
Introduced by Daniel Mayer Selznick

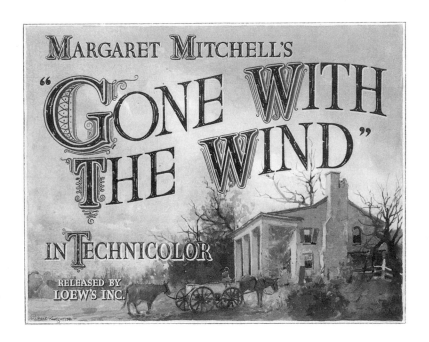

PRENTICE
HALL
EDITIONS

New York   London   Toronto   Sydney   Tokyo

Prentice Hall Press
15 Columbus Circle
New York, NY 10023

LC No. 89-062289

ISBN: 0-13-046740-5

Creative Staff: J. C. Suarès, Patricia
Fabricant, and Jane Martin

Manufactured in the United States of
America

10 9 8 7 6 5 4 3 2 1

First Edition

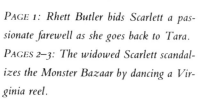

PAGE 1: *Rhett Butler bids Scarlett a passionate farewell as she goes back to Tara.*

PAGES 2–3: *The widowed Scarlett scandalizes the Monster Bazaar by dancing a Virginia reel.*

FRONTISPIECE: *16-year-old Scarlett runs away from the Tarleton twins.*

PAGE 5: *Watercolor painted by Wilbur Kurtz for use in advertising trailers prior to the release of GWTW.*

ABOVE LEFT: *Scarlett and Rhett during the No More Babies scene in Scarlett's bedroom.*

ABOVE CENTER: *Director Victor Fleming with Vivien Leigh before her entrance to Ashley's surprise party.*

ABOVE RIGHT: *Rhett drags Scarlett out of bed for the party and chooses her most brazen dress.*

RIGHT: *Green velvet negligée with sequin trim and taffeta lining, worn over a cream silk nightgown.*

OPPOSITE: *Wine velvet embroidered evening gown, with bead and ostrich trim.*

Contents

INTRODUCTION
A Member of the Family
by Daniel Mayer Selznick

ABOVE: *David Selznick with sons Danny and Jeffrey, taken in 1940.*
OPPOSITE: *David Selznick, age 11.*

S ince my brother Jeffrey was seven at the time *Gone With the Wind* was made, he got to go to the Selznick Studio to watch the filming of the famous pullback shot, where the camera rises to reveal an entire Atlanta street full of wounded soldiers. Not me. It was about the time of my third birthday, and I had to stay home. Searching through family papers to discover some hint of my state of mind at that time, I came across a letter from Laurence Olivier that read, in part: "Vivien remembered you, I am sure, as I do, when *GWTW* was in the making, as a very very small boy indeed—not rebellious about going to bed, but remarkably and touchingly sad about it."

As a child I had to wait a long time to find out what all the excitement was about. It wasn't until I entered kindergarten that I started hearing about the epic my father had apparently made. All my teachers and the parents of other children talked about the picture in awe: "Did your father really make *Gone With the Wind?*" No one could believe he thought I was still too young to see it. ("Not till you're ten," he'd say, and "old enough to appreciate it.) I tried to be patient about it, but secretly I was furious: It seemed an eternity before my tenth birthday would arrive.

When it did, on May 18, 1946, I managed to corral a boisterous group from my class at Beverly Hills' El Rodeo Elementary (along with some stragglers from Mattson's Boys Club) into the private projection room at the studio. A few parents and governesses came, too; every seat was taken. At the beginning, every member of the audience restlessly waited for the picture to start, but before the intermission several of my friends had dozed off: It *was* a long picture. I do remember, though, that when the words "The End" appeared on the screen, everybody cheered.

LEFT: *Selznick produced* King Kong *for RKO in 1933. His ingenuity was severely tested when he was forced to trim the budgets of other projects to keep the movie, with its expensive new technologies, going. Shooting took place on a locked soundstage to prevent disclosure of the new methods being used.*

RIGHT: Rebecca (1939), *with Joan Fontaine.*

As the lights went up the producer-host appeared at the door, waiting to greet every one of my friends. "Did you like it?" he asked. One girl's answer was unexpected: "It was awfully sad," she complained. "Why did so many people have to die?" My father burst out laughing. "They all died in the book, too," he explained, as if that were an acceptable defense to a ten-year-old.

When everyone had left my father put his arm around me. "Well, Danny boy, are you happy now?" It was a question he would suddenly utter at the oddest moments, but this time, after having experienced four hours of dazzling sights and sounds, my answer was ready. I told him it was the most wonderful picture I'd ever seen—certainly worth waiting ten years to see.

For my father, being a parent was no different from being a producer: He had unlimited enthusiasm for both. Choosing the perfect dentist was just as important as choosing the perfect costume designer—in fact, more important. No problem was too small, no decision too trivial. He always wanted you to know there were alternatives. You bought the wrong suit? No problem, we can take it back. You chose the wrong school? No problem, we can change it. Or, rather, *he* could change it.

A great teddy bear of a man, Dad had flat feet and long, strong hands that were always holding cigarettes about to drop ashes on his trousers. If he occasionally drove everybody crazy, he more than made up for it—with his generosity, compassion, and a sense of humor that extended even to joking about himself. He loved to laugh and make you laugh with

him. He could tell the same joke over and over in different company, each time roaring with delight as if he had never heard it before.

He was a man of many smiles, all tobacco-stained. His smile of disarming warmth greeted someone for the first time, while its more expansive and extended version was saved for old friends (followed by a grin and a hug). His mock-humble smile appeared when he was being complimented on one of his pictures; his guilty smile accompanied a fib (both smiles were exceptionally convincing). An astonished smile met an unexpected present or a surprise visit to the office by one of his three children. Later in life the sight of my half sister Mary Jennifer could light him up like a Roman candle. There was also a quick, tight smile that masked fear or anxiety—at which times my father found it impossible to accept help, except from a small circle of intimates. I'm told this smile appeared increasingly during the making of *Gone With the Wind.*

In 1935 Dad started Selznick International Pictures. Running a growing business along with personally producing several pictures a year (with the great care and taste for which he was already becoming celebrated) didn't leave him much time for family. Newspaper clippings reveal, however, that this hyperactive producer arrived at Hollywood's Cedars of Lebanon Hospital at seven o'clock on the night of May 18, 1936, just in time for my mother, ever the accommodating wife, to give birth to me. Shooting for the day had conveniently ended an hour earlier on *The Garden of Allah,* Selznick International's second film and also the

RIGHT: Intermezzo (1939) was Leslie Howard's next picture after GWTW. Ingrid Bergman's first screen test for David Selznick was made on the set of the library of Twelve Oaks.

second one made by Hollywood in three-strip Technicolor. (Its other virtues included Marlene Dietrich, Charles Boyer, a large supply of camels, and lots of sand.) That same week his eastern story editor, Kay Brown, urged him to buy Margaret Mitchell's voluminous manuscript, which was to be published that fall. He wouldn't agree to do so for another six weeks. From the correspondence available now, it's safe to say that he had no idea how much this seemingly small decision would change his life.

In 1986, when my older brother Jeff and I received the go ahead to make our documentary on *Gone With the Wind*, Dad had already been dead for twenty-one years. We found ourselves in the unenviable position of reconstructing the facts from our father's files and a handful of witnesses, some with shaky memories. What we learned, though, astounded both of us:

1. This picture finished principal photography at the end of June 1939, and was ready to be previewed with a temporary score—in a four-and-a-half-hour cut, no less—ten weeks later, in mid-September. (A comparable picture today would spend a minimum of six to eight months in postproduction.)

2. The full score was actually written and recorded from September to November of the same year.

3. Theaters all over the world agreed to book a film 222 minutes long, and no one would dream of removing a frame from *Gone With the Wind* for any of its return engagements. (Other Hollywood features of excessive length, such as *Cleopatra* [1963] and *Ben-Hur*

[1959], while allowed to play their original engagements without cuts, were subsequently drastically edited.)

Looking back, Jeff and I realized that *GWTW* was something of a family enterprise. First, there was Uncle Myron—more of the manic Selznick energy, but in a man half a foot shorter and with a lot less hair. He was Hollywood's talent agent to end all talent agents (or begin them: Some credit him with having invented the 10 percent cut), and he loved selling his clients to his brother for more money than any other lot in town would pay (he alternately called my father a genius and a chump). By the fall of 1938 he probably thought he had the market cornered on candidates for the role of Scarlett O'Hara, with both Joan Bennett and the indisputably charming Paulette Goddard under contract. (Unfortunately, Paulette lived across the street from us, which didn't make things any easier when my father wanted to announce he had finally found the winner of his two-year, worldwide search for Scarlett.) But Uncle Myron had one more ace up his sleeve—a long shot who happened to be the very talented girlfriend of his new, romantic client, Laurence Olivier. Very English, very delicate, and very cunning, Vivien Leigh knew she had only one opportunity to knock Myron's brother off his feet. Uncle Myron picked the perfect occasion—the burning of the Atlanta train yards on the backlot—to introduce her to his increasingly desperate brother, and Vivien made the most of it.

If my uncle delivered a Scarlett O'Hara, it took my grandfather to come up with a Rhett Butler. On the whole Dad's relationship with my mother's father,

Louis B. Mayer, was very good. Mayer ran MGM just down the street from Dad's studio, and Dad had been given his own unit at MGM from 1933 to 1935, after two banner years at RKO. However, I can't imagine Grandpa wanting to deny him the opportunity to create his own studio, or not wanting to assist with its biggest project. MGM's Clark Gable was, mind you, the only Rhett Butler readers of the book had ever wanted. Gable, though, wasn't exactly thrilled at being traded up and down Culver City's Washington Boulevard. He didn't want the part.

Needless to say Grandpa found ways to make it worth Gable's while. Moreover, MGM agreed to put up a million and a quarter (initially considered half the cost of the film) in exchange for the right to distribute it and divide the profits. But MGM's role didn't end there. When my father found himself at odds with his first director, George Cukor (who, among his other sins, was straying from Dad's script), Grandpa pulled Victor Fleming, Gable's buddy and favorite director, off *The Wizard of Oz* (leaving King Vidor to finish it) and assigned him to *Gone With the Wind*. He then found another movie for Cukor (the eminently suitable *The Women*, featuring, among others, Paulette Goddard) the week after he'd been fired. Swift and stylish.

George Cukor was family too—one of the two men my brother and I called "uncle" all our lives, aside from our real uncles. Between 1931 and 1935 he had directed five of Dad's pictures: *Bill of Divorcement, What Price Hollywood, Little Women, Dinner at Eight,* and *David Copperfield.* Except for my father, Uncle George was the most highly energized and galvanizing

personality of my childhood, with an explosive sense of humor. His reputation for directing "female" pictures and his superb visual sense must have made him seem a natural for *Gone With the Wind.* He worked on every aspect of the project for its first two years, including preparing and directing dozens of screen tests on a scale unprecedented in film history. Finding himself suddenly at odds with his closest friend—my father—after shooting had begun must have stunned him. It took its toll on Dad, too, but he quickly realized that he had to make a painful decision—and then went on to make even greater demands of Victor Fleming. Dad wanted to give Cukor a directing credit along with Fleming and the two other men who did considerable work, Sam Wood and production designer William Cameron Menzies. But neither they nor Fleming would hear of it. Years would elapse before Uncle George's considerable contribution to the film was publicly acknowledged.

The other "uncle" was John Hay Whitney, Selznick International's distinguished board chairman, who always seemed to me slightly larger than life. A Long Island millionaire who not only invested part of his own fortune—and that of his sister, Joan Payson—in Dad's new company, he persuaded other eastern money to come aboard as well. The only man my father was obliged to consult on financial matters, Uncle Jock reputedly kept Dad from indulging the great extremes to which he was temperamentally inclined. His relationship with *Gone With the Wind* began when he threatened to buy Margaret Mitchell's manuscript for Pioneer (the other film company in which he invested)

Elaine Hammerstein

Eugene O'Brien

Olive Thomas

Owen Moore

Elsie Janis

SELZNICK
PICTURES

Create Happy Hours

All America Loves the Beautiful

QUALITY impresses you on every hand in the stately mansion of George Washington at Mount Vernon.

Americans are quick to recognize quality, now as in the days of Washington.

To gain the respect of the American public through quality alone has always been the single aim of Selznick Pictures.

That is why they are to be found at theatres of highest standards.

That is why you feel as if you had been associating with a charming and intelligent friend, as you leave the theatre where Selznick Pictures create happy hours.

Lewis Selznick

AT THEATRES WHERE QUALITY RULES

LEFT: Selznick produced King Kong *for RKO in 1933. His ingenuity was severely tested when he was forced to trim the budgets of other projects to keep the movie, with its expensive new technologies, going. Shooting took place on a locked soundstage to prevent disclosure of the new methods being used.*

RIGHT: Rebecca (1939), *with Joan Fontaine.*

As the lights went up the producer-host appeared at the door, waiting to greet every one of my friends. "Did you like it?" he asked. One girl's answer was unexpected: "It was awfully sad," she complained. "Why did so many people have to die?" My father burst out laughing. "They all died in the book, too," he explained, as if that were an acceptable defense to a ten-year-old.

When everyone had left my father put his arm around me. "Well, Danny boy, are you happy now?" It was a question he would suddenly utter at the oddest moments, but this time, after having experienced four hours of dazzling sights and sounds, my answer was ready. I told him it was the most wonderful picture I'd ever seen—certainly worth waiting ten years to see.

For my father, being a parent was no different from being a producer: He had unlimited enthusiasm for both. Choosing the perfect dentist was just as important as choosing the perfect costume designer—in fact, more important. No problem was too small, no decision too trivial. He always wanted you to know there were alternatives. You bought the wrong suit? No problem, we can take it back. You chose the wrong school? No problem, we can change it. Or, rather, *he* could change it.

A great teddy bear of a man, Dad had flat feet and long, strong hands that were always holding cigarettes about to drop ashes on his trousers. If he occasionally drove everybody crazy, he more than made up for it—with his generosity, compassion, and a sense of humor that extended even to joking about himself. He loved to laugh and make you laugh with him. He could tell the same joke over and over in different company, each time roaring with delight as if he had never heard it before.

He was a man of many smiles, all tobacco-stained. His smile of disarming warmth greeted someone for the first time, while its more expansive and extended version was saved for old friends (followed by a grin and a hug). His mock-humble smile appeared when he was being complimented on one of his pictures; his guilty smile accompanied a fib (both smiles were exceptionally convincing). An astonished smile met an unexpected present or a surprise visit to the office by one of his three children. Later in life the sight of my half sister Mary Jennifer could light him up like a Roman candle. There was also a quick, tight smile that masked fear or anxiety—at which times my father found it impossible to accept help, except from a small circle of intimates. I'm told this smile appeared increasingly during the making of *Gone With the Wind.*

In 1935 Dad started Selznick International Pictures. Running a growing business along with personally producing several pictures a year (with the great care and taste for which he was already becoming celebrated) didn't leave him much time for family. Newspaper clippings reveal, however, that this hyperactive producer arrived at Hollywood's Cedars of Lebanon Hospital at seven o'clock on the night of May 18, 1936, just in time for my mother, ever the accommodating wife, to give birth to me. Shooting for the day had conveniently ended an hour earlier on *The Garden of Allah,* Selznick International's second film and also the

RIGHT: Intermezzo *(1939) was Leslie Howard's next picture after* GWTW. *Ingrid Bergman's first screen test for David Selznick was made on the set of the library of Twelve Oaks.*

second one made by Hollywood in three-strip Technicolor. (Its other virtues included Marlene Dietrich, Charles Boyer, a large supply of camels, and lots of sand.) That same week his eastern story editor, Kay Brown, urged him to buy Margaret Mitchell's voluminous manuscript, which was to be published that fall. He wouldn't agree to do so for another six weeks. From the correspondence available now, it's safe to say that he had no idea how much this seemingly small decision would change his life.

In 1986, when my older brother Jeff and I received the go ahead to make our documentary on *Gone With the Wind*, Dad had already been dead for twenty-one years. We found ourselves in the unenviable position of reconstructing the facts from our father's files and a handful of witnesses, some with shaky memories. What we learned, though, astounded both of us:

1. This picture finished principal photography at the end of June 1939, and was ready to be previewed with a temporary score—in a four-and-a-half-hour cut, no less—ten weeks later, in mid-September. (A comparable picture today would spend a minimum of six to eight months in postproduction.)

2. The full score was actually written and recorded from September to November of the same year.

3. Theaters all over the world agreed to book a film 222 minutes long, and no one would dream of removing a frame from *Gone With the Wind* for any of its return engagements. (Other Hollywood features of excessive length, such as *Cleopatra* [1963] and *Ben-Hur*

[1959], while allowed to play their original engagements without cuts, were subsequently drastically edited.)

Looking back, Jeff and I realized that *GWTW* was something of a family enterprise. First, there was Uncle Myron—more of the manic Selznick energy, but in a man half a foot shorter and with a lot less hair. He was Hollywood's talent agent to end all talent agents (or begin them: Some credit him with having invented the 10 percent cut), and he loved selling his clients to his brother for more money than any other lot in town would pay (he alternately called my father a genius and a chump). By the fall of 1938 he probably thought he had the market cornered on candidates for the role of Scarlett O'Hara, with both Joan Bennett and the indisputably charming Paulette Goddard under contract. (Unfortunately, Paulette lived across the street from us, which didn't make things any easier when my father wanted to announce he had finally found the winner of his two-year, worldwide search for Scarlett.) But Uncle Myron had one more ace up his sleeve—a long shot who happened to be the very talented girlfriend of his new, romantic client, Laurence Olivier. Very English, very delicate, and very cunning, Vivien Leigh knew she had only one opportunity to knock Myron's brother off his feet. Uncle Myron picked the perfect occasion—the burning of the Atlanta train yards on the backlot—to introduce her to his increasingly desperate brother, and Vivien made the most of it.

If my uncle delivered a Scarlett O'Hara, it took my grandfather to come up with a Rhett Butler. On the whole Dad's relationship with my mother's father,

Louis B. Mayer, was very good. Mayer ran MGM just down the street from Dad's studio, and Dad had been given his own unit at MGM from 1933 to 1935, after two banner years at RKO. However, I can't imagine Grandpa wanting to deny him the opportunity to create his own studio, or not wanting to assist with its biggest project. MGM's Clark Gable was, mind you, the only Rhett Butler readers of the book had ever wanted. Gable, though, wasn't exactly thrilled at being traded up and down Culver City's Washington Boulevard. He didn't want the part.

Needless to say Grandpa found ways to make it worth Gable's while. Moreover, MGM agreed to put up a million and a quarter (initially considered half the cost of the film) in exchange for the right to distribute it and divide the profits. But MGM's role didn't end there. When my father found himself at odds with his first director, George Cukor (who, among his other sins, was straying from Dad's script), Grandpa pulled Victor Fleming, Gable's buddy and favorite director, off *The Wizard of Oz* (leaving King Vidor to finish it) and assigned him to *Gone With the Wind*. He then found another movie for Cukor (the eminently suitable *The Women*, featuring, among others, Paulette Goddard) the week after he'd been fired. Swift and stylish.

George Cukor was family too—one of the two men my brother and I called "uncle" all our lives, aside from our real uncles. Between 1931 and 1935 he had directed five of Dad's pictures: *Bill of Divorcement, What Price Hollywood, Little Women, Dinner at Eight,* and *David Copperfield*. Except for my father, Uncle George was the most highly energized and galvanizing

personality of my childhood, with an explosive sense of humor. His reputation for directing "female" pictures and his superb visual sense must have made him seem a natural for *Gone With the Wind*. He worked on every aspect of the project for its first two years, including preparing and directing dozens of screen tests on a scale unprecedented in film history. Finding himself suddenly at odds with his closest friend—my father—after shooting had begun must have stunned him. It took its toll on Dad, too, but he quickly realized that he had to make a painful decision—and then went on to make even greater demands of Victor Fleming. Dad wanted to give Cukor a directing credit along with Fleming and the two other men who did considerable work, Sam Wood and production designer William Cameron Menzies. But neither they nor Fleming would hear of it. Years would elapse before Uncle George's considerable contribution to the film was publicly acknowledged.

The other "uncle" was John Hay Whitney, Selznick International's distinguished board chairman, who always seemed to me slightly larger than life. A Long Island millionaire who not only invested part of his own fortune—and that of his sister, Joan Payson—in Dad's new company, he persuaded other eastern money to come aboard as well. The only man my father was obliged to consult on financial matters, Uncle Jock reputedly kept Dad from indulging the great extremes to which he was temperamentally inclined. His relationship with *Gone With the Wind* began when he threatened to buy Margaret Mitchell's manuscript for Pioneer (the other film company in which he invested)

OPPOSITE: In this publicity still, Rhett comforts Scarlett after her bad dreams. CENTER AND RIGHT: Magazines put Clark Gable as Rhett and Vivien Leigh as Scarlett on their covers.

if Selznick International didn't want it. It was only when Dad learned that Whitney would buy it that he realized he'd better not let *GWTW* get away.

All family ties were put to the test in January and February of 1939, after Victor Fleming, who had just been named director, declared the script unfit to shoot. Production came to a halt for seventeen days as Ben Hecht went to work, retrieving the original Sidney Howard treatment and making it the basis of his own rewrite. Meanwhile the meter on the cash register continued to run to the tune of $10,000 a day, for which the company's bank accounts were not prepared. The studio was also simultaneously preparing *Rebecca* (Dad's first picture with Alfred Hitchcock) and an American remake of the Swedish *Intermezzo*, featuring its star Ingrid Bergman in her first English-language role. Naturally my father turned to his original backers, including MGM. *Gone With the Wind*'s budget would eventually swell to the then-astronomical figure of $4 million, more than $60 million in today's equivalents. Was MGM graciously prepared to increase its investment? It was not: For Grandpa, a deal was a deal. He'd bought a 50 percent interest in the film for $1.25 million and he would keep it without investing a dollar more. A last-minute rescue came from, yes, Uncle Jock and his sister Joan, who pledged a further million of their own money and put their signatures on a $1.5 million Bank of America loan— not only to finish *Gone With the Wind* but to finance *Rebecca* and *Intermezzo* as well. Clearly a commitment of this scale went beyond business. Nothing could have been a greater confirmation of their faith in my father.

No one reconstructing these events today is likely to recognize the increasing risk this venture must have represented in 1939. Granted, the book was a runaway bestseller. But this great, seemingly shapeless mass that kept postponing production soon became the laughingstock of Hollywood. After *So Red the Rose*, Civil War pictures were considered box office poison. And when Vivien Leigh was cast, Hedda Hopper publicly took my father to task and warned him that "people will stay away in droves." An *English* actress to play a Southern femme fatale? Was he out of his mind? Even after the successful previews, radio columnist Jimmie Fidler insisted the picture had "no chance to earn its money back," declaring it "irresponsible" to spend "two or three million dollars" on a single picture." During the shooting, when Victor Fleming was offered a small participation in lieu of additional salary, he replied, "Do you think I'm a damn fool? This is the biggest white elephant of all time." "Selznick's folly," they called it.

No wonder that my father reportedly behaved like a man on the edge of a precipice, sleeping less and less each night. Thank God my mother was there, encouraging, supporting, and believing in him and the film, too. Could either of them have predicted the outcome? I doubt it. Mother's memoir, *A Private View*, gives an uncompromising look at the film's human cost; by the time I too was old enough to understand Dad's habits the damage had been done.

As I grew up, I would ask Dad about *Gone With the Wind*, but he never seemed to want to talk about it

much. I always thought it was because everyone else badgered him to death about it, until one day I learned a possible reason: He had sold all his rights in the film—far too early, for far too little.

In August of 1942, tax attorneys advised him that it would be a good idea to sell both *GWTW* and *Rebecca*, his following film (and, incidentally, the Oscar winner for 1940), and take capital gains on them. *The Wind* had by then played all over America and in many countries throughout the world, though not yet in continental Europe or Japan, the "war zones." This was before the days of television, and certainly long before the word *videocassette* had even entered the vocabulary. It's not hard to reconstruct what might have been his state of mind at the time: Here was a film that no one thought had a chance of recovering its astronomical cost, and Uncle Jock and Joan Payson were prepared to hand him a substantial check for it. No waiting around for Lord-knows-how-many more years of war (postponing income from those countries), no waiting to see how the picture would do in reissue. My mother was appalled. Uncle Myron called him a chump, insisting that he would *never* sell *his* 3 percent of the film. (Indeed, that small piece has poured millions into Uncle Myron's estate since his death in 1944.) Still, Dad was elated, but not for long.

Only a few months later he tried to buy back at least some of what he had sold, but it was useless: Jock Whitney had resold it to MGM for five times the price. Uncle Myron was one of the few original investors who had shares left, and after his death, my father, while looking after his brother's estate, moni-

tored incoming checks from MGM obsessively. Believing the studio to be guilty of cheating on a film from which the company had already made "excessive profits," he took after it with a passion worthy of Don Quixote. Not until 1953, four years after Margaret Mitchell's death, did he finally acquire a piece of *The Wind* again: the novel's film and television rights. When he resold much of this back to MGM some ten years later for a handsome profit, he considered himself at least partially vindicated.

Though he continued to make a number of very fine films, including *Since You Went Away* and *Portrait of Jennie*, he remained preoccupied with *GWTW*. " 'Fiddle-dee-dee'—can't you just imagine it?" he said to me excitedly when I was home one weekend from college. "It's a perfect opening number." It seems he had decided to produce a lavish Broadway musical called (what else) *Scarlett!* "What about Rodgers and Hammerstein? "What about Frank Loesser?" I didn't understand why he would want to compete with himself, but trying to stop my father's enthusiasm about anything was like to trying to halt Niagara Falls. "Why should I let anyone else do it?" was his answer. "I know the book better than anyone, I know the construction problems, I understand these characters. I can write the dialogue myself and get financing from ten different sources." As usual his arguments were irrefutable. But when I learned he was considering Leroy Anderson (composer of "Syncopated Clock") for the score, I became alarmed. "What about Max Steiner?" I pleaded, "Everyone loves his music for the film." Dad thought the suggestion predictable, point-

OPPOSITE: *Another family portrait from 1940. Selznick with sons Jeffrey, 8, and Danny, 4.*

ing out that I had no idea what was at stake (which was true; how could I?). Later, he moved on to pursuing Dimitri Tiomkin. Fortunately, he finally abandoned his plans for this venture, although a similar production did come to pass (with a score by Harold Rome) in Tokyo, London, and Los Angeles. Why he had changed his mind I never learned, but my father could talk himself out of things as easily as he could talk himself into them.

The single occasion when he was prepared to devote himself wholeheartedly to the subject of *GWTW* in later years was during the Civil War centennial in Atlanta in 1961, when for one weekend the city had the chance to pretend it was 1939 again. Vivien Leigh was flying in from London, and Olivia De Havilland was coming from Paris. Sadly, Clark Gable would be absent—he had died on the set of *The Misfits* the year before. When Dad asked me to join him on the trip I jumped at the chance.

My father went through the weekend's events almost too eagerly, posing for pictures, shaking lots of hands, and signing countless programs. For once he could forget the issue of who sold what percentage to whom.

The first night's ball was like a Hollywood fantasy of the Old South: hundreds of hoop skirts whirling and curtsying, mint juleps being passed around on every tray, Confederate flags on all the walls. Vivien looked radiant and elegant in a way that made everyone keep his distance—as if in the presence of a queen. Olivia, looking just as regal, simply inspired the kind of affectionate tenderness the world came to associate with the character of Melanie.

The next night, the Grand Theater (site of the original première) was once again graced with the facade of Twelve Oaks, ablaze with searchlights, and surrounded by crowds that screamed and cheered every few minutes even if no celebrities were arriving. Inside, with Vivien seated between my father and myself and Olivia sitting right in front of us, I felt immensely privileged. Dad was already ducking out for cigarettes, which he would do several times, and Vivien smiled nervously for the photographers who ran up and down the aisle popping their flashbulbs ceaselessly. I found myself staring at her: She looked especially vulnerable. Could it have been the fact that her marriage to Laurence Olivier was ending after all those years, or was my imagination working overtime? I smiled at her and she smiled back, instantly reminding me of the Tenniel drawing of the Cheshire cat in *Alice in Wonderland*. Like the Cheshire's, Vivien's was a face that held many secrets.

The picture started, the titles welcomed onto the screen by a roar from the audience. Suddenly, Vivien took my hand; only then did I realize she'd been trembling. When Rhett Butler appeared at the bottom of the Twelve Oaks stairs—in that startling close-up shot from Scarlett's point of view—the crowd burst into applause. "Oh Clark!" Vivien cried. "He was so young, I can't believe he's gone."

Four short years later my father would be gone too, and two years after that, Vivien herself. As she watched her younger image with alternating waves of

laughter and sadness, she seemed to be reliving a thousand memories. I would have given anything to know what they were.

With the final shot of Scarlett under the tree, the audience began what would become a deafening roar of appreciation. Vivien wrapped her hand around my father's arm and squeezed. "Oh David," she said, sounding exactly like the young Scarlett, "it's still so wonderful."

"So are you," said my adoring father, "so are you."

Slowly, the three figures rose to acknowledge the continuing ovation, a spotlight focused on them. The smile on my father's face at that moment was the fullest I had ever seen: clearly, he was overcome.

Vivien blew kisses to the balcony, and Olivia and my father waved and waved. And then suddenly Dad turned to me. I knew what was coming. "Danny boy, are you happy?"

This time I didn't have to answer. I realized at that moment that it didn't matter to my father whether he owned the picture anymore or not. It had long since staked its claim on him in other ways—like a distant relative who is invited to dinner and stays a lifetime. *Gone With the Wind* had become a part of all our lives: my grandfather's, my uncle's, and even mine. The movie I had not been old enough to watch being made had slowly crept up on all of us and became a member of the family.

CHAPTER ONE
Margaret Mitchell

RIGHT: *Margaret, age 4, with kitten, Atlanta, 1904. From a very early age much of her childhood would be spent listening to the family's tales of the Civil War.*

LEFT: *Maybelle Stephens Mitchell and her children, Margaret, age 6, and Stephens, age 11, Atlanta, 1907. To encourage her daughter to read, Maybelle gave Margaret 15 cents for every novel she read. OPPOSITE: In the doorway of 1149 Peachtree Street, 1920.*

I chose the Civil War to write about because I was raised on it. As a child I listened for hours on Sunday afternoons to stories of fighting in Virginia and Georgia, to the horror of Sherman's approach, his final arrival and the burning and looting, and the way the refugees crowded the trains and the roads to Macon. And I heard about Reconstruction. In fact I heard everything except that the Confederates lost the war. When I was ten years old, it was a violent shock to learn that General Lee had been licked. And I thought it had all happened just a few years before I was born.

—MARGARET MITCHELL

OPPOSITE: Margaret Mitchell as an Atlanta Journal reporter, 1923.

RIGHT: The Fitzgerald plantation in Clayton County, Mitchell's maternal grandparents' home and inspiration for Tara. The plantation was pillaged during the Battle of Jonesboro, but the family saved its valuables by burying them outside.

The long road leading to Margaret Mitchell's immortal story, *Gone With the Wind,* began when her ancestor, William Mitchell, left South Carolina to become the first Mitchell in Georgia in 1834. His son Isaac, a farmer and Methodist minister, moved with his family to Atlanta in 1856 and performed the first wedding ceremony in the city. Isaac's son Russell Crawford Mitchell became the first lawyer in the family. He joined the Confederate army, and after being seriously wounded at the Battle of Sharpsburg in 1862 became the ward master of an Atlanta hospital, and then the owner of a successful lumber business. His first son, Eugene Muse Mitchell, also took up law, becoming quite prominent in Atlanta. He secured the $145,000 grant from Andrew Carnegie to build the Atlanta Public Library, where daughter Margaret would later do most of her research for *GWTW.* He also organized the Atlanta Historical Society in 1926 with Franklin Garrett and Wilbur Kurtz, both of whom would be instrumental in helping Margaret check the facts in her manuscript. Kurtz went on to become the historical consultant for the production of Selznick's picture.

But Eugene Mitchell's most fortuitous accomplishment may have been winning the hand of Mary Isabel "Maybelle" Stephens, a gentle, devout, and strong woman who helped to found the Atlanta women's suffrage movement. She was not only descended from the stormy Irish stock that produced the fictional O'Hara family, but her mother, the fiery Annie Fitzgerald, stole away her sister Sarah's beau, John Stephens, married him, and helped him run a wholesale grocery business in Atlanta. Annie's childhood had been spent on a large farm in rural Georgia. Her father, Philip Fitzgerald, had been forced to leave Ireland, and her saintly mother, Eleanor, had been transplanted (as Ellen O'Hara was) from a civilized area—in this case Maryland—onto a sprawling, unlovely plantation. Like Tara, the Fitzgerald farm raised only daughters, and like Tara, it was plundered by Union soldiers after the war.

Margaret Mitchell was born in her grandmother Annie's house in Atlanta on November 8, 1900. Here she first encountered the family's rich legacy of oral history—countless retellings of the Civil War, a Southern obsession that continued to be fought over and over again in family arguments, tales, and legends passed down by Maybelle.

Margaret's was an idyllic childhood. On a pony that could jump a little but balked at bars, and which she could ride well by the age of five, she would take frequent rides with her "boon companion," a Confederate cavalry veteran, and go through make-shift "maneuvers" with several of his friends, finishing the days with rousing arguments about the war. She also read avidly (Dickens, Thackeray, biographies of Confederate heroes, *Grimm's Fairy Tales*, almost anything in the Carnegie library); took dancing lessons, which she loved; and wrote constantly. She and her friends presented her plays in the massive front room of Eugene Mitchell's new house on Peachtree Street.

As she grew older she was gradually exposed to the harsher realities of life. In the aftermath of the great fire of May 1917, which devastated a hundred Atlanta blocks (including eleven of Annie's houses), Margaret volunteered at the refugee center and witnessed scenes of unbelievable dislocation and despair. That year also ushered in the next incarnation of war-time Atlanta. Margaret came of age during World War I in the fascinating and fascinated company of the young officers her brother Stephens brought home from nearby Fort McPherson. The summer was full of parties and dances at the Mitchell home, the Capitol City Club roof garden, and the elegant Piedmont

Driving Club. Margaret fell in love with Clifford West Henry, a dashing army lieutenant, who gave her an engagement ring before she left for her first year at Smith College. She made the trip north with her mother, and they stopped at the Henry house in New York. But in October Margaret received the news that Clifford, who had shipped off to war with her brother Stephens, had been mortally wounded in France. Then in January 1919 she received word that her mother, whom she hadn't seen since the trip to Smith, was severely ill with Spanish influenza, and things had taken a turn for the worse. Margaret was summoned home and arrived only to find her mother had died the day before. With her father gripped by a bereavement from which he would never recover, Margaret stepped in to run the faltering household at the end of the school year in June.

Living at home with a dependent father and a critical grandmother (Annie) was less burdensome for Margaret than it might have been. During the 1920–21 season she was a debutante, although she was a bit too daring for staid Atlanta society. At a charity ball she performed a risqué Apache dance, and was punished by being omitted from the Junior League's roster of invitations for membership. While relishing a tweak at the noses of Atlanta society, she had probably expected to be protected by her family's good name.

At an August costume dance Margaret met Red Upshaw, whose life paralleled somewhat that of her later creation, Rhett Butler. Berrien K. Upshaw ("Red" for his hair) was from a good North Carolina family (Rhett's family was from South Carolina) and was expelled from Annapolis Military Academy in Sep-

tember 1920 (Rhett was expelled from West Point). He made money as a bootlegger (Rhett was a war profiteer). His wildness and lack of gentility appealed to the rebellious Margaret. Stung by the Junior League's rejection, she reacted with characteristic defiance, becoming more and more involved with Red. Their courtship had an excitement and an aura of latent danger, and Margaret was smitten. They married in September 1922 and moved into a suite of rooms in the Mitchell house. But the union began to disintegrate almost immediately. Red was unable to support Margaret and he lost control of his drinking. His behavior toward her bordered on being abusive.

Witness to much of this was Kentucky-born John Marsh. He had come to Atlanta in 1920 to work as a reporter for the *Atlanta Georgian* and had wound up sharing an apartment with Red. They had the same friends, and John also courted Margaret Mitchell, who won his heart with her warm, flirtatious manner. It was for her sake rather than Red Upshaw's that he agreed to be best man at their wedding. A 1916 graduate of the University of Kentucky and a World War I veteran, he was as safe as Red was dangerous, as modest and considerate as Red was moody and passionate. At Margaret's request, he came down from his job in Washington, D.C. to help repair the marriage, but he was too late. The Upshaws had already decided to divorce, and in December Red coldly and dispassionately informed Margaret that he was taking a job in North Carolina, and walked out. Margaret, with a tragic engagement and a broken marriage behind her at the age of twenty-two, was deeply shaken.

John Marsh provided a strong arm for her to lean on. With his help she got a job at the *Atlanta Journal Sunday Magazine* at $25 a week and wrote her first story on December 31, 1922. It was the only job she would ever have, and it went a long way toward preparing her to write *GWTW*. During her six-day, sixty-hour work week, she wrote articles on more or less lightweight subjects, but she did so with such talent and energy that she was soon the magazine's top writer. Editor Angus Perkerson was impressed that she came in early (not like a late-rising deb), opened the office, worked hard, took any story, and wrote "like a man," without requiring much editing. With John Marsh's continuing support and advice, Margaret's faith in herself grew.

In 1923, she reported on Rudolph Valentino's visit to Atlanta, where he was judging a local beauty contest. In the midst of a contract dispute with Paramount, he had been forced to go on the road and perform anywhere but inside movie theaters to make money. Margaret interviewed him on the roof of the Georgian Terrace Hotel. As the great star lifted Margaret (4'11" and 90 pounds) back through the window into the building, she dropped her purse, pulled out the hem of her skirt as she bent to pick it up, and bumped heads with him as he stooped to help. Despite the slapstick, the interview did much to boost her career. (Coincidentally, David O. Selznick made his first movie of another beauty contest Valentino was judging in Madison Square Garden during the same tour, and the movie made him a $15,000 profit.)

In July 1923, still basking in the glow of Valentino's visit, Margaret returned to her rooms in the house on Peachtree Street to find Red Upshaw waiting for her. She made the mistake of inviting him in. When she

LEFT: *Lake Burton, Georgia, 1920.*
RIGHT: *As a debutante, Margaret shunned the usual staid portraiture in favor of free-style poses.*

refused his demand that she fulfill her wifely duty to him, he beat her so severely that she had to be hospitalized. By promising not to prosecute him, she was able to secure a divorce in June 1924. In December John Marsh suffered an attack of the hiccups that lasted forty-two days. Upon his recovery, he and Margaret became engaged and were married on July 4, 1925.

Margaret's first home of her own was their new apartment, christened "The Dump" because it was small and dark. Free of her censorious father and her critical grandmother, Margaret created a literary salon of unmatched quality in Atlanta. She filled "The Dump's" two rooms with the witty, the intelligent, and the high-spirited—most lured by Margaret's wit, her stories, and her exuberance. The conversation was stimulating and often centered around literary questions. In May 1926, Margaret quit her job at the *Journal* which she had promised to do when John received a raise and a promotion. With plenty of free time, she worked on a column, research projects, short stories, and even started a novel titled *Ropa Carmagin*. But late that year she badly twisted an ankle she had injured twice before. She became bedridden with arthritis. To pass the long hours she read the books that John would fetch from the library. When he finally tired of all the back-and-forth, he brought her home a stack of typing paper and told her that she'd better write her own book.

She made her first efforts at *GWTW* while she was on crutches. Every day she would plant herself at her small portable typewriter set up by the only window in the apartment that provided any light. She finished the last chapter first and then set out to fill in the details. As the years passed, she never let her friends know what she was doing and hid her work whenever someone came by. John was her only sounding board, though a highly effective one. With no title and a heroine named "Pansy O'Hara," the novel was finished but for three chapters by 1929. Margaret let it stand incomplete when she began to recover the ability to walk without crutches, leaving it in a huge stack of envelopes, the untidy evidence of three years of concentrated, painstaking work.

In 1932, when the Marshes moved to a larger apartment down the street from the Peachtree mansion to be near the ailing Eugene, Margaret resumed sporadic work on the manuscript, fleshing out characters, adding details, and researching events. This would be her last peaceful period.

In April 1935, Harold Latham, a Macmillan vice-president, came to the South in search of prospective novels and was introduced to Margaret Mitchell. She insisted that she had nothing to give him, but her bashfulness piqued his curiosity. He knew from his associate editor in New York, Lois Cole, that a novel existed. When he broached the subject a third time, he brought up something that struck in Margaret's mind: The reason no one knew about the South was that no Southern writers had come forward with a decent portrayal of Southern life. She still politely rebuffed him, but when she got home she talked it over with John Marsh. "It couldn't do any harm," he said with characteristic understatement, to have someone professional take a look. In a letter to John Marsh's mother she wrote what she did next:

I had no intention of parting with the book and I told [Harold Latham] so when I said good-bye at

RIGHT: *Medora Field Perkerson* (center) *with the staff of the* Atlanta Journal Sunday Magazine. *She introduced Margaret Mitchell to Harold Latham of Macmillan.*

about six o'clock. He was leaving at seven-thirty. But between the time I left him and seven-thirty something happened which made me good and mad for the first time in ten years, and I decided to give it to him after all and get a rejection slip. So I tore home and tried to collect the manuscript. For years it has been knocking around the house in twenty very dirty manila envelopes. Some were under the bed and I had to crawl in after them. Some were in the top of the pot and pan closet. I got dusty under the bed and greasy in the closet. I had no first chapter or rather sixty first chapters each worse than the other, so I sat down and tore off a first chapter. By then it was seven o'clock. I rushed to town and it wasn't until I was in the lobby of his hotel that I realized what I looked like: hatless, hair flying, dust and dirt all over my face and arms, and worse luck, my hastily rolled stockings coming down about my ankles. As I went toward him in the lobby, I kept dropping envelopes and finally had three bellboys picking them up behind me. I couldn't pull up my stockings as my hands were occupied but Mr. Latham was a perfect gentleman and he kept a perfectly straight face and acted as though all authors looked like me. The poor man was already packed and his taxi was waiting and he had nothing to carry the twenty envelopes in and was forced to buy a please-don't-rain suitcase from a bellboy to pack the stuff in.

"Here," she'd said, handing him the novel, "take this before I change my mind."

"It was one of the worst-looking manuscripts I had ever seen," Latham would later comment, but he was enchanted by the story. He took it back to New York and by August the contract was signed. Margaret had only eight months to prepare the manuscript, finish chapters, add characters, find the historical data to back up her story line, and disguise all the real names and places she had used. She asked Atlanta historian Wilbur Kurtz to proofread two chapters with descriptions of the battle of Atlanta, and she consulted Franklin Garrett about the name Watling. "She wanted assurance that the name wasn't among pioneer citizens of Atlanta," Kurtz recalled. She also consulted her brother Stephens's articles in the *Atlanta Historical Bulletin*; pored over old newspapers, diaries, and letters; and spent hours in the library checking facts. John took a month off work to help her edit. Macmillan didn't like the name Pansy for her heroine, so they settled on Scarlett. Margaret wrote several more first chapters until she finally found one she liked. Concerning the matter of a catchy title, Margaret wrote to Latham in August 1935 about a phrase from an Ernest Dowson poem: "The more I think of it, the more I'm inclined to 'Gone With the Wind.' It has movement, it could either refer to times that are gone like the snows of yesteryear or things that passed with the wind of the war or to a person who went with the wind rather than standing against it. What do you think?"

The name stuck. She returned the manuscript to Macmillan in February 1936. Its first notice appeared in a February 6 column in the *Atlanta Constitution*, and in April the Book-of-the-Month Club made *GWTW* its July selection. Margaret, who had been hoping for five thousand copies to be sold at least in the South, ". . . went to bed ill with an ice pack on [her] head and aspirin every half hour."

The book was unofficially released on May 5, 1936, and Macmillan sent copies to all the major studios. In just a few months Margaret Mitchell would be vaulted clear out of the ranks of private citizenry and into the unending difficulties of public life.

She would never write for publication again.

CHAPTER TWO
The Producer

He [Selznick] said to me rather impolitely that to pay $50,000 for a book, the author of which nobody had ever heard of, was crazy, and was I crazy. No, I said, I wasn't crazy at all, he was the crazy one, and we had a very good-natured argument about the whole thing and he said "How do you know it's gonna sell?" I said, "I know it's gonna sell!" "How do you know it's gonna sell?" he said again. Well, I couldn't answer that question, you see, so we left it rather at an impasse, and I said, "If you don't buy this book this afternoon, I won't be responsible because we're gonna lose it." And he said, "I'll think about it."

—KAY BROWN

OPPOSITE: DOS in his office at Selznick International, 1939, under the ever-present photograph of his father, Lewis J. Selznick. OVERLEAF: Selznick expresses his trepidations to Kay Brown, May 25, 1936.

TO KB FRM DOS   May 2[...]

HAVE GONE OVER AND CAREFULLY THOUG[...]

WIND."   THINK IT IS FINE STORY A[...]

IT.   IF WE HAD UNDER CONTRACT A W[...]

WOULD PROBABLY BE MORE INCLINED TO[...]

THAT ITS ONLY IMPORTQNT SHOWMANSHI[...]

CASTING   OR IN A TREMENDOUS SALE[...]

FOR IT NOW IN THE HOPE WE COULD GE[...]

HOPE BOOK WILL HAVE TREMENDOUS SAL[...]

OF THE LARGER COMPANIES CAN AFFORD[...]

EXPECTATION OF SUCH CASTING OPPORT[...]

FEEL WE CAN TAKE SUCH A GAMBLE.   I[...]

I KNOW YOU WILL WATCH ITS$ SALES [...]

BECOME AN ANTHONY ADVERSE A- WHIC[...]

DRESGMTBLN VOLCRBE, INEABUSLOBAVEO[...]

936

BOUT " GONE WITH THE

I ~~UNE~~ UNDERSTAND YOUR FEELING ABOUT

N IDEALLY SUITED TO THE LEAD, I

YIT THAN I AM TODAY BUT I DO FEEL

ALUES WOULD BE IN EITHER SUCH STAR

CA

THE BOOK.   TO PAY A LARGE PRICE

UCH A STAR AND-OR IN THE FURTHER

S I FEEL/UNWARRANTED.   PERHAPS ONE

Y IT NOW IN THE HOPE OR ~~EXOECTATION~~

TIES AND SUCH A SALE BUT I DO NOT

T IS NOT PURCHASED IMMEDATELY THEN

FULLY AND IF IT THREATENS TO

OWEVER I FRANKLY DOUBT- THEN WE

EGRETS OTHER COMPANELBUNCIDENTALEY

Macmillan was asking $100,000 for the movie rights to *Gone With the Wind*. At Selznick International, the novel was received by Kay Brown, who was in charge of the New York office. In an era when women's roles behind the camera in the movie industry could be severely limited, hers was crucial. "I was responsible for calling important material to his attention," Brown later recalled, "and I thought this book was sensational." Selznick, hard at work in California on *The Garden of Allah*, hardly shared her enthusiasm. Thus began one of the most persistent campaigns in motion picture history—in the form of memos, telegrams, messages, and phone calls—as Kay Brown, witnessing the storm the book had set off in New York, mounted her urgent (and effective) effort to convince Selznick to buy the rights.

Selznick had known Brown since their days at RKO, which he'd been hired to run in late 1931. Only three years old, RKO had been established by David Sarnoff—who owned the patent to the Photophone, a movie sound device—to take advantage of the introduction of the talkies. Sarnoff was not a member of the movie "Old Guard," a system that disgusted Selznick.

Selznick's first task at RKO was to reorganize the giant operation—a network of facilities starting with the studio and ending with 250 theaters—into a productive unit, and then begin RKO's rejuvenation. By the time he finished, he had recruited director George Cukor from Paramount; produced his first milestone, *Symphony of Six Million* (1932), the first movie with a full-length score by Max Steiner; produced *A Bill of Divorcement* with Katharine Hepburn, who was signed at Cukor's insistence, and *Bird of Paradise* with Dolores Del Rio (both 1932); reduced the studio's expenses by more than 25 percent (without compromising his standards of quality); plucked Fred Astaire off the stage and signed him up; and made the 1933 blockbuster, *King Kong*. As he would reflect years later, in 1958, "They were the great pioneering days, the great frontier days. Everything was 'The First,' and when sound came in, everything became new all over again. We were all pioneers—everything we did had never been done before."

It was also during these years that he honed the producer's skills for which he would become famous: handpicking his crew and staff with fastidious care, hiring people for what they could do and not who they were, and involving himself in every aspect of a movie's production, which he did increasingly via memo. Even then he could unleash a torrent of memos: instructing, questioning, reproving, praising, conceptualizing. He dictated them day and night, exhausting both his secretaries, writing them on any kind of paper he could find. They were dreaded, welcomed, loathed, and sometimes appreciated, but anyone who worked for him came to accept them as a fact of life.

The memos were a sign of his need for total control, not for ego's sake as much as for the sake of a movie. "A motion picture is like a painting," he had insisted to his employers at Paramount in 1930 (before leaving for RKO). "Instead of oil paints, it uses talents and personalities to tell its story. But each artist must paint his own picture and sign it."

In 1933, he took that doctrine with him to MGM, stepping in for the ailing Irving Thalberg at the request

```
WANT YOU TO NOTE THAT I HAVE THOUGHT FURTHER ABOUT "&GONE WITH THE WIND"
AND THE MORE I THINK ABOUT IT THE MORE I FEEL TERE IS EXCELLENT PICTURE
IN IT STOP  SUGGEST YOU CALL THIS TO MR COOPERS AND MR WHITNEYS
ATTENTION FOR PIONEER AS POSSIBLE COLOR PICTURE ESPECIALLY IF THEY
CAN SELL THE VERY COLORFUL MANS ROLE TO GARY COOPER STOP    WERE I WITH
MGM I BELIEVE I WOULD BUY IT NOW FOR SOME SUCH COMBINATION AS GABLE AND
CRAWFORD STOP
END  LS
```

of his father-in-law, Louis B. Mayer. The studio's immense resources enabled Selznick to bring to the screen the great classics he'd been brought up reading—*David Copperfield, A Tale of Two Cities, Anna Karenina.* There were other successes as well—*Dancing Lady* and *Dinner at Eight*—but the experience of making screen versions of novels that were complex and difficult to condense taught Selznick lessons that came in handy for *Gone With the Wind*: Stick to the spirit of the book, follow its plot as closely as possible, maintain authenticity, and find the right actors.

Selznick International Pictures had been running for a year (backed by John Hay Whitney, Irving Thalberg and his wife, Norma Shearer, and David's brother Myron) when Kay Brown received Mitchell's novel from the Macmillan agent. On its backlot in Culver City, California, nicknamed "40 Acres"—with eleven sound stages and seven theaters leased from RKO-Pathé—David Selznick had already produced the successful classic *Little Lord Fauntleroy* and was in the process of making another, *The Garden of Allah* (much of it shot in the Arizona desert). It was a vehicle for the new Technicolor process, a proviso Whitney had attached to his financial support because he owned a large chunk of Technicolor. Though the film cost an astronomical $1.5 million and did not break even, Whitney was satisfied with the experiment. The next film to come out of SIP would be the masterful *A Star Is Born*, a resounding success and arguably Selznick's finest film thus far, followed by two that filled the theaters but did not make Selznick a profit: *The Prisoner of Zenda* and *Nothing Sacred*, the latter made at Whitney's suggestion. When Selznick returned to the familiar, more comfortable ground of classic adaptations with *The Adventures of Tom Sawyer*, the film flopped.

A substantial motion picture was needed that would assuage any doubts in the minds of Selznick's investors—a vehicle for the studio's success. Kay Brown needed only one read to recognize *Gone With the Wind*'s potential as a movie and less than two weeks to prepare a fifty-seven-page synopsis of the story (sent to Selznick on May 20, 1936). "Is synopsis in DOS's hand yet?" she cabled Marcella Rabwin, Selznick's assistant.

I'm really steamed up about this book and every minute counts STOP There is going to be keen competition for this picture one company has already made an offer of $25,000 STOP I would appreciate it if you would read this synopsis immediately and advise me of your reactions STOP I think that this is an absolutely magnificent story and it belongs to us STOP There are four main character parts the title role of Scarlett is made-to-order for Miriam Hopkins or Betty [sic] Davis STOP Melanie should be played by Janet Gaynor Rhett by Clark Gable STOP My feeling is the price will be fifty thousand dollars STOP You can see that I'm absolutely off my nut about it and I would appreciate your notifying me the minute the synopsis has arrived and when I might expect to hear from you.

Selznick, who had put off reading the synopsis while he was distracted by the problems of other projects, initially felt it was too much of a gamble. The book's sales, meanwhile, rose amid universally positive reviews.

PIONEER SELZNICK

TO KB FROM SS

JULY 7,1936

DOS ON SET   FOLLOWING HIS REPLY

IF YOU CAN CLOSE "GONE WITH THE WIND" FOR 50,000 DO SO STOP ALTERNATE

PROPOSITION 5500 AGAINST 55,000 FOR 90 LOR 60 DAY OPTION STOP I

REALIZE THERE IS NOT MUCH CHANCE OF YOUR BEING ABLE GET THIS ON

OTPIONAL BASIS BUT YOU MIGHT MAKE A STAB AT IT AS I WOULD PREFER THIS

IN ORDER TO HAVE OPORTUNITY DETERMINE HOW COULD CAST IT ET C STOP

ON OUTRIGHT PURCHASE REGRET INABILITY TO PAY MORE THAN 50,000

BUT I FRANKLY THINK THIS, WHICH IS MUCH HIGHER PRICE THAN HAS BEEN

APID FOR ANTHONY ADVERSE AND OTHER IMPORTANT BOOKS, IS AS HIGH ZAS

WE SHOULD GO IN VIEW OF FACT THAT EVEN IF BOOJK JUSTIFIES THE

HIGHEST HOPES THAT ARE HELD FOR IT IT COULD NOT BRING MUCH MORE MONEY

AND 50,000 WOULD BE EXCELLENT PRICE VEN IN SUCH CIRCUMSTANCES

THEREFORE IN ADVACNCE OF PUBLICATION I CANNOT SEE MY WAY CLEAR TO

PAYING ANY MORE THAN 50,000 STOP KNOW HOW HARD YOU HAVE WORKED ON

THIS AND HOPE THIS WILL NOT MEAN OUR LOSS OF PROPERTY BUT IF IT

DOES IT JUST CANT BE HELPED STOP YOU MAY ASK WHAT DIFFERENCE AN

EXTRA FIVE OR THEN THOUXXXTEN THOUSAND DOLLARS WOULD MKE ON A PROPERTY

LIKE THIS BUT THE POINT IS THAT I FEEL WE ARE EXTENDING OURSELVES

CONSIDERABLY EVEN TO PAY SUCH A PRICE FOR IT IN VIEW OF FACT THAT

THERE IS NO CERTAINTY WE CAN CAST IT PROPERLY

END DOS SS

MIN

OK WILL CALL YOU BACK IN ABOUT FIFTEEN MINS

EKB

*OPPOSITE: July 7, 1936
RIGHT: Katharine "Kay" Brown ("KB"
on memos), SIP's New York representative,
who kept a close watch on the literary scene
in her search for potential screen properties.
GWTW was her finest coup.*

With RKO bidding on it as a vehicle for Katharine Hepburn, Brown turned to Jock Whitney (who loved the book) for help. He told Selznick that he would buy it himself if Selznick didn't; Selznick, not wanting to be second-guessed, authorized Brown, via a telegram sent by Marcella Rabwin, to bid $50,000. "You are sure there is no mistake," the frantic Brown cabled back.

"Absolutely," replied Rabwin.

"Hold your seat I've closed for fifty thousand dollars," responded Brown. Selznick was still on the set of *The Garden of Allah*, watching the last rehearsal. He would not get to read the book until his vacation in July 1936.

Selznick returned from his vacation to an office hip-deep in 8 × 10 glossies, telegrams, letters, and messages from actresses and agents. With the announcement that he had purchased the motion picture rights to Mitchell's novel, virtually every actress in Hollywood over the age of fourteen was coveting the role of Scarlett O'Hara. But casting Scarlett was only one of the problems Selznick was grappling with. Even with a supremely creative crew of hardworking artisans at his disposal, *Gone With the Wind* would be a massive risk.

Selznick International Pictures was completely out of step with the way the major studios operated in 1936. The average American would go to the movies about thirty-six times that year. In 1936, there were 130 million Americans; the average yearly wage was $1,700; admission cost 25 cents, which would be equivalent to about $3.50 today. Approximately 18,000 theaters were selling a total of 90 million tickets per week (or 5,000 tickets per theater). The big studios were run like factories, releasing in total ten new features every week. Double features were the rule, and motion pictures seldom ran more than ninety minutes. By the end of 1936, SIP had released just two movies of this length.

There was also the stigma of *Anthony Adverse*, released that year. The novel was about the same length as *GWTW*, and only its first half had been filmed, running 2¼ hours. Reviews labeled it an ill-conceived attempt to cram too much material into too little time. Selznick would be trying to put an entire book into that same running time, and already the fan mail was stacking up demanding that he be absolutely true to Mitchell's story and leave nothing out.

But Selznick did have the strong backing of John Hay Whitney, who believed in Selznick's policy of eschewing the security of formula pictures in favor of high-quality production. The two men saw *GWTW* solely in epic, Technicolor terms. So the producer took his first giant steps toward initiating *GWTW*'s production. To untie the Gordian knot of finding a screenplay within the novel's 1,037 pages, he hired Sidney Howard in October 1936, "the best constructionist around right now," paying him $22,500 for a finished script. He convinced George Cukor, who had just finished directing Greta Garbo in *Camille* and Leslie Howard and Norma Shearer in *Romeo and Juliet*, to tackle *GWTW*, even with no production date in sight. To keep *GWTW* before the public until it could be finished, he dispatched SIP's publicity director, Russell Birdwell, an ace Hollywood publicist and an ex-reporter and motion picture writer, to launch a

publicity campaign so all-inclusive and so well planned that even the most cynical denizens of Hollywood would become willing participants, sucked in by its sheer intensity and volume.

United Artists had the release rights to all SIP features until December 1939, which is precisely when *GWTW* wound up ready for distribution. If Selznick wanted to distribute his blockbuster on his own, or if he foresaw having to negotiate away distribution rights for the loan of a major star, he could have had Birdwell keep the publicity mill rolling until the end of that year. Also, allowing some time to pass between the publication of the book and the movie's release would make the details and plot twists a bit dimmer in the public's mind, and abridgments less noticeable. Though Selznick wanted to film the entire novel, he knew radical cuts would be called for. That the "Great Search for Scarlett" lasted as long as it did was probably no accident.

And what of the talent search itself, with its fairy-tale ending of Selznick himself finding the perfect Scarlett at the last minute? Early favorites for Scarlett included Bette Davis, Katharine Hepburn, Miriam Hopkins, Tallulah Bankhead, and Norma Shearer, but Selznick wanted to prevent (at almost any cost) *GWTW* from deteriorating into a "star vehicle," and becoming known as a "Davis picture" or a "Hepburn picture." What he really needed was a relatively unknown face, with enough talent and experience to carry the movie. So whether or not the search was in earnest, Birdwell began it with a vengeance, involving more than a hundred talent scouts spread across the country, countless radio and newspaper announcers, hundreds of hopeful Scarletts, and an unabashedly opinionated public.

Suddenly, everyone was a casting expert, not only for Scarlett but for the other characters as well. Eleanor Roosevelt wrote personally, to recommend her maid for the role of Mammy. Newspapers published lists that included Ronald Colman, Basil Rathbone, Errol Flynn, Gary Cooper, and Clark Gable for the part of Rhett Butler. Selznick dispatched Kay Brown to organize the hunt, and every well of talent in the country was plumbed, including high school drama departments. She took director Tony Mann (to shoot the screen tests) and her secretary south in December 1936. In Atlanta she put a notice in the paper inviting Scarlett hopefuls to come to the Biltmore lobby the next morning and was awakened by a call from the lobby desk: There were one thousand people waiting downstairs. Margaret Mitchell came to the rescue with fifteen members from the Junior League. Brown recalled an encounter with a man with a pistol: " 'I want to play Rhett Butler,' " he said, and I said, 'I'll see to it!' And I went out and called the police."

Out of the hundreds of belles and debutantes who thought they were Scarlett and dozens of mammies who knew they were Mammy, five or six were considered for an audition. Cukor made a follow-up tour in March 1937 with assistant casting director John Darrow and interiors designer Hobe Erwin (who would be replaced by Joseph Platt), looking not only for talent but for locations. Ultimately, the only performers the trips to the South turned up were girls chosen for minor parts, primarily because they were Southern:

Alicia Rhett, Mary Anderson, and Marcella Martin (whose lines would have to be dubbed because she didn't sound Southern enough). Back in Hollywood, Selznick and Jock Whitney worked on the plan of casting an unknown by offering countless girls screen tests while out on the town. It kept the SIP secretaries swamped, but proved fruitless.

By the beginning of 1939, the Scarlett Search would involve 1,400 prospects and ninety screen tests at a cost of $92,000, using more than 142,000 feet of black-and-white film and 13,000 feet of Technicolor. But even by early 1937, when no one—not even Selznick—knew when filming would begin, the production estimates exceeded $2 million. Whitney would subsidize not only this outlay but also Selznick's takeover of the entire "40 Acres" complex he'd been leasing from RKO-Pathé. The public's overwhelming insistence that Clark Gable play Rhett Butler was gradually forcing Selznick to consider more financial concessions, since Gable's boss (and Selznick's father-in-law), L. B. Mayer, was driving a hard bargain.

CHAPTER THREE

Preproduction

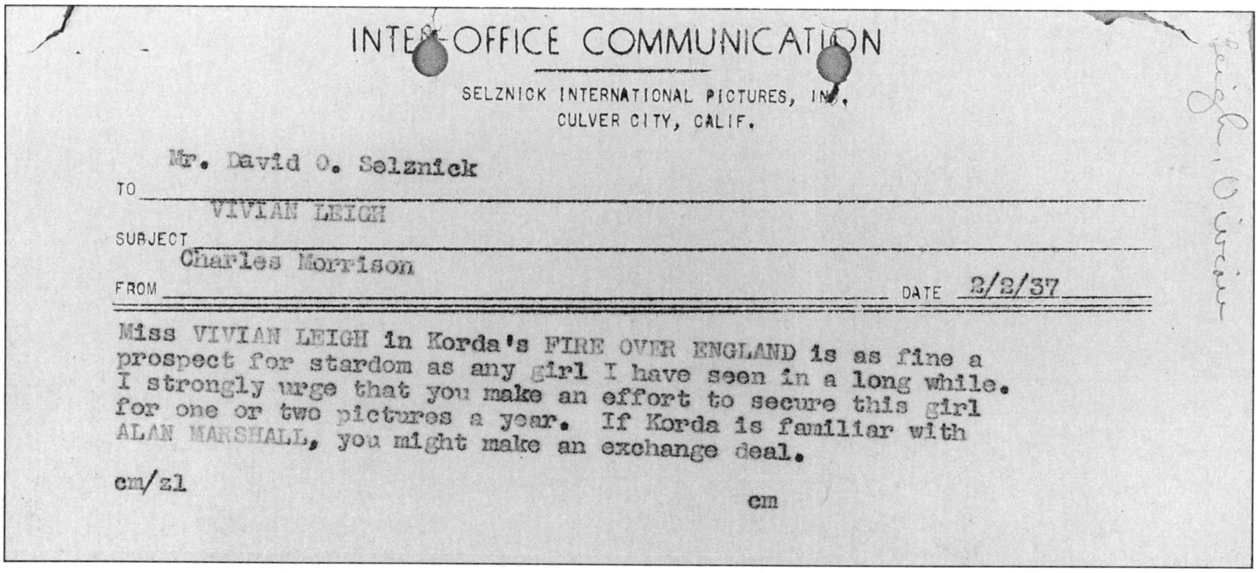

INTER-OFFICE COMMUNICATION

SELZNICK INTERNATIONAL PICTURES, INC.
CULVER CITY, CALIF.

TO _Mr. David O. Selznick_

SUBJECT _VIVIAN LEIGH_

FROM _Charles Morrison_   DATE _2/2/37_

Miss VIVIAN LEIGH in Korda's FIRE OVER ENGLAND is as fine a
prospect for stardom as any girl I have seen in a long while.
I strongly urge that you make an effort to secure this girl
for one or two pictures a year. If Korda is familiar with
ALAN MARSHALL, you might make an exchange deal.

cm/zl

                                   cm

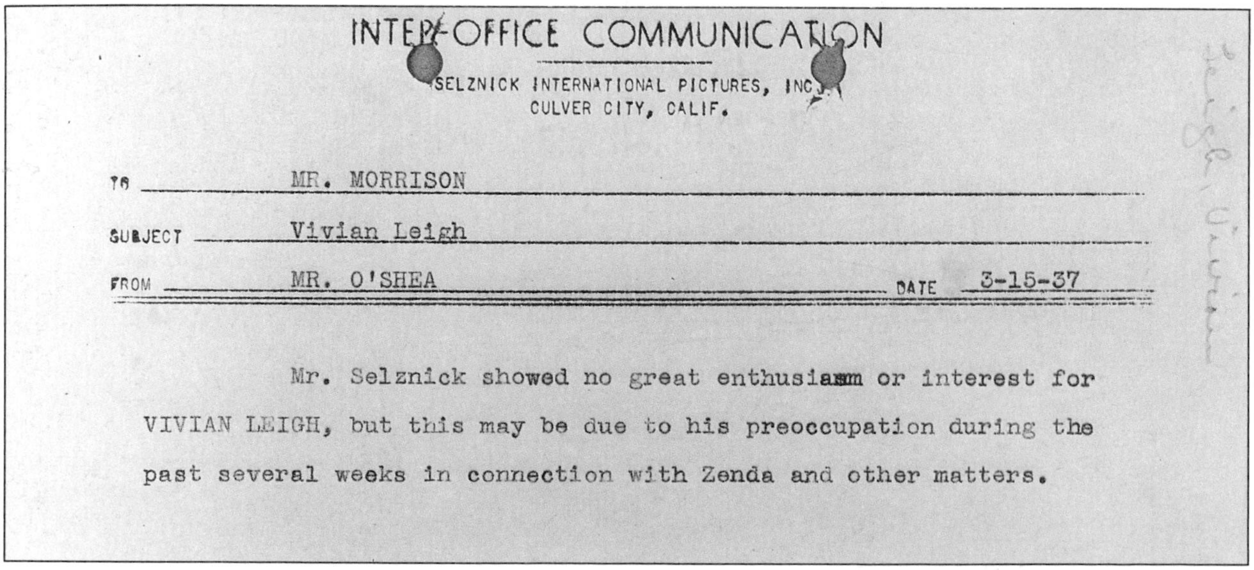

INTER-OFFICE COMMUNICATION

SELZNICK INTERNATIONAL PICTURES, INC.
CULVER CITY, CALIF.

TO _MR. MORRISON_

SUBJECT _Vivian Leigh_

FROM _MR. O'SHEA_   DATE _3-15-37_

Mr. Selznick showed no great enthusiasm or interest for

VIVIAN LEIGH, but this may be due to his preoccupation during the

past several weeks in connection with Zenda and other matters.

OPPOSITE: Vivien Leigh in Fire Over England.

Throughout the middle months of 1938, Selznick was still trying to hammer out a script with Sidney Howard, spending up to five hours a day looking for a screenplay of workable length. Hal Kern, SIP's supervising film editor, had already estimated that the screenplay in its fifth draft would require a five-hour picture. Short of splitting *GWTW* into two features, that was unacceptable.

But the problem was not solely Howard, a talented Pulitzer prize–winner with countless scripts to his credit. An impeccable reputation for turning out quality work under deadline enabled him to make his own rules, including his refusal to work in Hollywood. He divided his time between a New York City home and a Massachusetts farm—a vexing situation for the control-obsessed Selznick. A first draft, finished within four months (on February 12, 1937), translated into a six-hour picture; to make the "radical amputations" Howard agreed were necessary, he took an April trip to Hollywood. Together he and Selznick cut seventy pages, beginning a complicated series of changes and revisions that continued through most of 1938. Selznick grew increasingly dissatisfied. Margaret Mitchell, who had at first firmly refused to answer Howard's technical questions—her policy was to stay out of the movie-making—found herself sympathetically offering advice.

The screenplay also faced the problem of the Production Code of 1933, which exercised strict control over the content of scripts, censoring anything that did not meet its standard of delicacy. In October 1937, censor Joseph Breen had written Selznick to strongly suggest that "any suggestion of rape or the struggles suggestive of rape" be removed; that "Rhett should not be so definitely characterized as an immoral, or adulterous man; the long scenes of childbirth should be toned down considerably; Scarlett should not offer her body to Rhett in the scene in the prison; and the character of Belle should not definitely suggest a prostitute." Breen continued, "Please be careful that, in scenes of undressing there be no undue exposure of the person of Scarlett; scenes of the dead or wounded are not too realistically gruesome, [nor are] the pain and suffering of childbirth; Ashley, Rhett, et al. are not shown as offensively drunk; and there is no suggestion that Rhett is about to rape Scarlett. . . . merely have him take her in his arms, kiss her, and then gently start with her toward the bedroom." He concluded with somewhat misguided praise: "In our judgment you have done a magnificent job with this first draft script. . . . More power to you!" Although Selznick would be able to avoid most of the Hays Office's attempted bowdlerizations of his script, the battle would continue until the very end.

The technical preparations for filming were also under way. William Cameron Menzies had been hired in mid-1937 to design the production and Lyle Wheeler was working on set design, lighting, and camera angles. Special effects wizard Jack Cosgrove was brought in to take care of trick photography, including matte shots, multiple exposures, process backgrounds, and incredibly detailed paintings. Production manager Ray Klune informed Selznick that with Cosgrove, "we no longer have any worry in connection with this phase of our work." A confident Selznick then told Henry Ginsberg, general manager of studio operations and the Bank of America's representative on SIP's staff, that "Cosgrove will be figuring out just what sections of sets he can save from having to be built, and just what effects he can give us that otherwise might be either unobtainable or too costly." Cosgrove's work, taking the place of elaborate sets (including a complete Twelve Oaks), would also save time.

The SIP research department, headed by Lillian Deighton, was not having as much success locating historically accurate materials, though Selznick was determined that authenticity be, for the most part, maintained, Mitchell, who refused to be pressed into service as a historical consultant herself, was adamant as Selznick on this point. "I took your name in vain today," she told Atlanta historian Wilbur Kurtz after suggesting him to the producer. She also recommended friend Susan Myrick: "Take her out to the Coast . . . to pass on the authenticity and rightness of this and that, the accents of the white actors, the dialect of the colored ones, the minor matters of dress and deportment, the small touches. Her grandpa, old General Myrick, had the biggest and whitest columned house in Georgia, at Milledgeville, and Sue is the youngest child of a Confederate soldier. She was raised up in the country and she's a commonsense, hardheaded person with an awful lot of knowledge about Georgia folks and Georgia ways, not only of this time but of times past." Concerning accents, she wrote Selznick that she and other Southerners preferred that the cast use their natural voices to that "bogus Southern talk they have heard on the stage and screen so often."

Others were worried about damaging portrayals in *GWTW*. Beginning in mid-1937, Selznick International was inundated with letters and newspaper and magazine articles protesting characterizations that writers found racist and degrading. Mitchell was accused of fostering a racial bias; sympathizing with lynch laws, slavery, the Ku Klux Klan; and denigrating both the black race and the Northern emancipators. There were calls to stop filming, threats to boycott all of Selznick's pictures. Selznick started negotiations with Walter White, secretary of the NAACP, writing in June 1938, "I hasten to assure you that as a member of a race that is suffering very keenly from persecution these days, I am most sensitive to the feelings of minority peoples." White replied that while he knew "Mr. Sidney Howard and his work and thus how sincere his interest in and attitude towards the Negro are, it will require almost incredible effort to make a film from the novel which is not both hurtful and an inaccurate picture of the Reconstruction era. I do not mean to stress racial chauvinism or hypersensitiveness. Our interest is solely that of accuracy."

As a compromise they agreed "that the picture should make no mention of the Ku Klux Klan and show no Negro violence . . . avoid offending Negro sensibilities; avoid any derogatory representations . . . and eliminate the major things in the story which were apparently found offensive by Negroes in the Margaret Mitchell novel . . ." Further, black characters would be written to allow them to maintain their dignity and the word *nigger* would be eliminated, but the speaking of dialect could be maintained for accuracy. With this uneasy truce the preparations for production continued.

The Scarlett search, meanwhile, was taking on a cultic atmosphere, although George Cukor got to use the screen tests as a means to see how his conceptions of particular scenes actually appeared. By mid-1938 Bette Davis had taken herself out of the running by appearing in *Jezebel* for Warner Brothers—her character's similarity to Scarlett was one attraction to doing the movie. Selznick was irked by the film's obvious resemblance to *GWTW*. Paulette Goddard moved to the head of the pack, but her candidacy would be doomed unless she could produce a marriage license legalizing her live-in relationship with Charlie Chaplin. Scarlett had to be virgin-pure, able to withstand the scrutiny of the press bloodhounds. Selznick reiterated his grand plan: Give the public a talented unknown, someone unassociated with any other picture.

The crew and technical staff were largely oblivious to this monkey business. Sidney Howard was still hard at work trimming his script (he would not give up until his death in August 1939). William Cameron Menzies was painting the scene concepts from which Lyle Wheeler would design the sets. Walter Plunkett was occupied with the 2,000 costumes and 5,500 individual pieces of clothing required. As film editor Hal Kern would help keep the running time reasonable: The plan was to edit as production went along. Will Price was coaching the Scarlett and Melanie candidates in Southern accents, and Monty Westmore's department was handling makeup and hairstyling for them all. Fred Parrish, the still photographer for SIP, was preparing to begin the monumental project of recording the entire production (it would turn out to be the most complete and detailed collection of still work ever done for any motion picture). Moving freely through the entire organization was a cheerful Wilbur Kurtz, on the lookout for historical anachronisms.

At the same time Selznick was becoming perturbed with the directorial situation. Disagreements over the approach to *GWTW* were already brewing between him and George Cukor, who was receiving $4,250 per week because he had not agreed to direct any other picture since early 1937. Selznick seriously considered switching to Victor Fleming. But Fleming went to work on *The Wizard of Oz* in late 1938, which removed him from contention, as it did a candidate for Carreen O'Hara—Judy Garland.

Casting continued. Selznick finally caved in and struck the inevitable deal with L.B. Mayer, securing Clark Gable's services. Gable's contract forced a start date of January 1939. Barely four months remained to round out the cast and technical staff and to finish enough of the sets and costumes to start production. Publicity angles were still being sought at every turn: Margaret Mitchell refused to allow Selznick to use any of her original manuscript for promotional purposes, claiming she had burned it. Ray Klune was ordered to make sure all props, sketches, miniatures, and schedules would be kept for use in future publicity campaigns. They were also slated to go on display at the World's Fair.

While Selznick went to Bermuda for two months to try to make something out of Howard's piles of notes and drafts with scriptwriter Jo Swerling, Ray Klune, Bill Menzies, Lyle Wheeler, and Wilbur Kurtz were occupied primarily with planning the scene that has erroneously come to be known as "the Burning of Atlanta." (It actually re-created the burning of Confederate munitions in the Atlanta train yards on September 1, 1864; Union General Sherman did not order Atlanta proper burned until November 14, 1864.) Carrying out Klune's idea of burning the old sets on "40 Acres" was a massive undertaking, the main problem being that only seven Technicolor cameras would be available on the night scheduled for the shoot (December 10, 1938) to film the tremendous amount of footage required. With the various takes it was figured that at least forty minutes of consecutive burning would be needed, but there was no way the flimsy wooden structures of the old sets would last that long. A miniature of the set was built, every movement was choreographed and rehearsed, every camera angle dissected, every detail probed to prevent wasting one shot. It would be a spectacle of a magnitude unmatched on film.

Lee Zavitz of the SIP special effects department solved the problem by providing a fire that could be turned on and off at will. Within every structure the Selznick crew laid two sets of pipes, one to carry a mixture of coal oil and kerosene and one to carry water. Both sets were connected to electrical pumps with shut-off valves, so the flow could be alternated. Zavitz had also provided for remote lighting via contact switches wired into the sets. The burn was set for 8 P.M. According to the call sheet, the two doubles each for Rhett and Scarlett, as well as the two drivers who would lie in the wagon beds, would rehearse at 1 P.M. A hot supper was planned for 5 P.M., and police and fire protection (almost forty pieces) arrived a moment later.

The care that went into this sequence can be noted in the attention to details. Ray Klune found the one stunt double in Hollywood who was closest to Gable in physical dimensions: Yakima Canutt, who had doubled for Gable before and had studied the actor's mannerisms. Klune even provided Canutt with Gable's actual costume, which was unused at that point (which meant that Gable would have to keep it spotless while filming until the point when the fire

scene occurred). When 8 P.M. finally rolled around, the crowd of two hundred was warned into absolute silence. The twenty-seven cameramen readied the seven monstrous cameras, and the doubles took their places. William Cameron Menzies ordered Lee Zavitz to set the fire and was rewarded with an instantaneous, glorious combustion. Zavitz's ingenious piping allowed for six or seven separate takes over ninety minutes, and on the last take a tractor pulled down the massive set that had once been the temple gates for *King Kong*. For less than $25,000, David Selznick's technical crew gave *GWTW* one of its most memorable sequences.

The fire scene also gave the world its Scarlett O'Hara: In a legendary meeting, Laurence Olivier's agent, Myron Selznick, presented Vivien Leigh to his captivated brother, David Selznick. David Selznick braced himself for a hurricane of criticism for having chosen an Englishwoman to play this thoroughly American role, but there was little complaining. Almost everyone except columnist Hedda Hopper thought she fit Margaret Mitchell's description of Scarlett to a tee: slim, sparkling, fiery, dark-haired, and green-eyed—thanks to the quick thinking of cameraman Ernest Haller (who used a yellow filter on her screen test to make her blue eyes come out right). Selznick even got the approval of the Daughters of the Confederacy: "Better an English girl than a Yankee."

Up until then, Mitchell had told Kay Brown she preferred not to see the screen tests of discarded Scarletts, perhaps afraid to be sucked into the selection process and thus into participating in the production, which she was still resisting. But she was pleased when Selznick airmailed her a film of Vivien's screen test as well as those of some minor characters, including that of Oscar Polk as Pork, in early January. She wrote Selznick on January 14, 1939, "No one with whom I have talked made any objections about Miss Leigh being English and not American." But she refused his entreaties to help him with the script, unwilling to pull his chestnuts out of the fire. "Don't get panicky at the seemingly small amount of revised script," Selznick was forced to write Jock Whitney on January 25, 1939. "It is so clearly in my mind that I can tell you the picture from beginning to end. As long as I survive, the whole situation is well at hand." His reassurance was perhaps more prophetic than he realized: Selznick would wind up rewriting much of the script himself, putting a great strain on *GWTW*'s budget.

OPPOSITE: George Cukor discusses a scene from Camille *(released by MGM in 1936) with Greta Garbo. "Cukor was an exceptional man," Ben Hecht, one of* Gone With the Wind's *scriptwriters, observed. "He didn't know anything, except one thing. He didn't know anything about stories, he didn't know anything about directing, sets, technique. He had a flair for women acting. He knew how a woman should sit down, dress, smile. He was able to make women seem a little brighter and more sophisticated than they were, and that was about the only talent he had."*

RIGHT: The primary GWTW scriptwriter, dramatist Sidney Howard, "only came to California to discuss the rewrites, then went home," said Kay Brown. "And that's the only man I've ever known Mr. Selznick ever to allow that privilege, but Sidney was Sidney and he just wouldn't do anything else. . . . He wouldn't go anyplace from his farm—he would write on his farm." Three years later, Ben Hecht was brought in to salvage the badly hashed-up script, on which everyone, it seemed, including F. Scott Fitzgerald and Selznick himself, had worked, and wound up using much of Howard's. Marcella Rabwin recalled, "In the end, whatever was left of anybody's work really was Sidney Howard's . . . [and] in the last analysis [Selznick] wrote the last script of GWTW. And wrote it under the most terrible circumstances, where he'd sit up all night long, and the people would come to the set in the morning, and there's nothing there, and Mr. Selznick was in his office still struggling away on a yellow scratch pad, and they're down there waiting for words. They can't shoot; it's costing money."

LEFT: *Mervyn LeRoy, Judy Garland, and GWTW's next director, Victor Fleming, with Toto, surrounded by the Munchkins on the set of* The Wizard of Oz, *MGM—1939. It was said that Fleming made* Wizard *for his two daughters and, similarly, it could be said he took over GWTW for Clark Gable. Fleming was not quite finished with principal photography for* Wizard *when he was asked to step in, so David Selznick closed down shooting for two weeks until he was free. In the evenings after a long day on GWTW, Fleming would return to MGM to edit* Wizard, *which put a severe strain on him.*

OPPOSITE: *Victor Fleming in 1928 as a Paramount director. He got his start as a cameraman: "I learned much from Douglas Fairbanks. We spent hours discussing the subject of camera techniques, agreeing that the camera can never fully tell a story standing still. Later, during the First World War, I filmed instruction pictures on gunnery for the army and I learned something more about the value of action pictures."*

OVERLEAF, LEFT: *The Queen of Hollywood for the moment, Clara Bow, with fiancé Victor Fleming on the set of* Rough Riders *in San Antonio, Texas, 1926. (They did not marry.) Selznick called Fleming "the most attractive man who ever came to Hollywood. Physically and in personality. He had a kind of Indian quality. American Indian, that is. Women were crazy about him."*

OVERLEAF, RIGHT: *Directing Jean Harlow in* Red Dust, *MGM—1932, with Clark Gable, the first time Gable worked with Fleming.*

ABOVE, TOP: *Selznick makes a deal with father-in-law Louis B. Mayer, who makes a deal with Rhea Langham, Gable's wife, who grants a divorce to Gable, who signs a contract for* Gone With the Wind. *"Mr. Selznick knew that Gable was Rhett Butler," recalled Marcella Rabwin, "but Selznick knew, too, that Gable did not want to do this picture and that Mr. Mayer was going to make a very tough bargain. Mr. Selznick had no luck with his relatives—they all exacted from him the 'pound of flesh.' He paid for Myron's clients much more than they had ever received before. But Mr. Mayer really had his eye on the*

film. . . . Gable's wife, Rhea, was adamant about not giving him a divorce so that he could marry Carole Lombard. [Mayer] finally came to David and said, 'I will give Rhea $500,000 if she will give him his divorce, on the condition that he make this film and that you give [MGM] half of it. I will supply you with completion funds [about $500,000].' . . . Mr. Selznick finally capitulated. To use [Gable] we had to make an enormous concession . . . the largest salary ever paid for an actor. We gave away half [of] the greatest, most productive, most lucrative film ever made."

CENTER, LEFT: *Gable with Greta Garbo in* Susan Lenox, Her Fall and Rise. *MGM honored their new leading man by pairing him with their premier female star for this one film.*

RIGHT: *Clark Gable with Leslie Howard, Lucy Beaumont, and Norma Shearer (in her trademark satin gown) in* A Free Soul *(MGM, 1931). Produced by Shearer's husband, Irving Thalberg, the film launched the careers of both Gable and Howard.*

OVERLEAF, LEFT: Red Dust, *in which Gable displayed the tough persona he developed earlier under the influence of Victor Fleming that would rocket him to stardom.*

OVERLEAF, RIGHT: *Gable and Carole Lombard. "I was scared when I discovered that I had been cast by the public," Gable said. "I felt that every reader would have a different idea as to how Rhett should be played." But, as Evelyn Keyes explained, "The people of the United States, if I can make a pompous statement, chose Clark Gable. . . . All the columnists, they'd discuss it on the radio . . . in the newspapers. There just wasn't anybody else who could play Rhett Butler and that was that." Early on, Carole Lombard was suggested for Scarlett, but refused to test for the role.*

LEFT: *The British actor Leslie Howard with Mary Pickford in* Secrets, *1933 (Pickford's final screen appearance). "American picture actresses are wonderful," Howard said. "They have studied their art and it is delightful to work with them. It was refreshing to work with Mary Pickford in* Secrets *and see the eagerness and ceaseless effort she put into the production. I didn't particularly care for my role, but for her sake gave it all I could."*

OPPOSITE: *With Norma Shearer in* Romeo and Juliet, *1936. "His career was a cool, highly technical achievement," said his son Ronald Howard, "and, unlike many theatrical careers, was supranormal rather than in any way abnormal or bizarre."*

Having already enjoyed some twenty years on stage and screen, Howard demurred when Selznick asked him to play young Ashley Wilkes, feeling he was too old for the part. Selznick was aware of his doubts, writing to Daniel O'Shea on October 20, 1938, "My worry about Howard is purely and simply concerning his age . . . Howard is an unusually intelligent actor, and I think that if it were explained to him that [we] simply have the necessity . . . of making sure that he is right pictorially, Howard would make this test . . . Nothing is as much a worry as the moment as the casting of Ashley, not even the casting of Scarlett." Howard ultimately made the test, commenting, "Money is the mission here, and who am I to refuse it?" Selznick sweetened the deal by offering Howard the chance to co-produce (as well as act in) Intermezzo after GWTW was finished.

LEFT: Olivia de Havilland in The Charge of the Light Brigade, *1936, her second film with Errol Flynn.*

OPPOSITE: Dodge City, *1939, one of five pictures Olivia de Havilland did with Errol Flynn between 1935 and 1939. Marcella Rabwin recalled her desire to be in GWTW: "Olivia de Havilland was under contract to Warner Brothers. They were not going to give her up. But Olivia was really smarter than all of them put together. One of her friends was Ann Warner, who was married to Jack. And Olivia went to Ann, and they sat down over lunch, and Olivia was crying and she said, 'They're making a big mistake, because if they let me play this part I'll be worth so much more to the studio! If they let me out, they can get so much more money for me. I will be a really important star! It's a terrific part!' Well, she sold Ann Warner, and Ann Warner called up Jack and said, 'You've got to let Olivia go!' And that was that!"*

RIGHT: A beaming Olivia de Havilland in her film debut as Hermia in Warner Brothers' version of A Midsummer Night's Dream, *with an all-star cast that included Jimmy Cagney and Dick Powell. De Havilland began her career playing Puck in the play produced by her drama coach, Dorothea Johnson, in 1934. When the European theatrical producer Max Reinhardt produced his spectacular version of* Dream *at the Hollywood Bowl, de Havilland wound up with the part of Hermia only a few days before opening night.*

Reinhardt's extravaganza was witnessed by L.B. Mayer, Clark Gable, and Hal Wallis, a Warner Brothers producer, among other luminaries. De Havilland, barely eighteen, made such an impression on Wallis that he insisted Jack Warner fly out to see her. Warner bought out her theatrical contract, choosing her for the film version after he decided Bette Davis was too big a star for the part. During production she already displayed the cheerful, selfless professionalism that would make her so popular on the GWTW set.

LEFT: *Hattie McDaniel in 1936, the seasoned performer:* "I had headlined on the Pantages and Orpheum circuits, but vaudeville was dead as last month's hit song. Milwaukee was really my springboard to Hollywood. I landed there broke. Somebody told me of a place as a maid in the ladies' room at Sam Pick's Suburban Inn. I rushed out there and took the job. One night, after midnight, when all the entertainers had left, the manager called for volunteer talent from among the help. I asked the boys in the orchestra to strike up 'St. Louis Blues.' I started to sing 'I hate to see the evening sun go down' . . . I never had to go back to my maid's job. For two years I starred in the floor show." *After a number of movie roles she read Mitchell's novel and was fascinated by the role of Mammy:* "I naturally felt I could create in it something distinctive and unique."

OPPOSITE: *Hattie McDaniel, age 15, photographed in Denver, 1910.* "I was little more than a kid, but I was old in show business. I won a medal in dramatic art when I was 15. One year later, my oldest brother, Otis, wrote his own show and songs, and persuaded my mother to let me go on the road with his company. I loved every minute of it, the tent shows, the kerosene lights, the contagious enthusiasm of the small-town crowds."

OPPOSITE: *Vivien Leigh in* Dark Journey, *1937. Selznick talent scout Charles Morrison had already pointed her out to Selznick in a February 2, 1937, memo, but the producer was too preoccupied with the early stages of* GWTW *to notice. Leigh, meanwhile, having read Mitchell's novel, informed her agent that she was ideal for Scarlett. He reminded her that Alexander Korda, the biggest moviemaker in Europe, owned her contract, and that the role was uniquely American. Vivien replied that she was French-Irish, like Scarlett, and that most inhabitants of the South were first- or second-generation English in the mid-19th century, convincing him to send Selznick photographs and reviews. After* Dark Journey *she returned to the stage for* Because We Must; *her opening night gifts to the cast were copies of* GWTW. *While filming* A Yank at Oxford *(1938), which would give her excellent exposure in America, she asked costar Robert Taylor what an American Southern accent sounded like. By summer 1938, she had four films running simultaneously in New York, all of which brought her favorable reviews.*

Among the more apocryphal tales about how Leigh was discovered is the story that Myron Selznick's assistant Nat Deverich (an ex-jockey) gave Daniel O'Shea a hot tip at Santa Anita, in return for which O'Shea quietly added Leigh's name to a routine list of actresses to be tested for Selznick. Allegedly, DOS signed the memo after only a perfunctory glance; he hadn't been thrilled with Leigh before. But the official story of how Leigh provided David Selznick with his Scarlett O'Hara at the last minute *is that she impetuously followed her lover, Laurence Olivier, to America to be with him for five days before returning to England for the play* A Midsummer Night's Dream, *and decided to stay after Olivier convinced his agent (Myron Selznick) to suggest her to DOS. A memo from Daniel O'Shea to Selznick dated December 8, 1938, starts: "This is just to remind you that Vivien Leigh is here. The [Myron] Selznick office handles her. They are talking deals for her on a picture basis. They want $22,500 per picture for her. I am trying to get her in to see George Cukor. She leaves for London at the end of the week." It was written two days before Atlanta was due to be burned, and the $22,500 fee is close to what she was offered to do* GWTW *($1,250 per week, for 16–20 weeks).*

At the filming of the burning of the Atlanta train yards, Vivien was presented to David by the light of the dying fire. "David, I want you to meet your Scarlett O'Hara," Myron said to his dazzled brother, who offered her a screen test immediately.

Wilbur Kurtz, the film's resident historian and an acute observer, wrote in his journal for December 10 that "a charming young lady appeared just before the fire sequences began, squired by a handsome chap. . . . I accosted Marcella [Rabwin, DOS's personal secretary] as to whom she might be. Marcella cupped a hand to her lips and whispered, 'Vivien Leigh. Mr. Selznick is seriously considering her.' Later, when Selznick walked off the set, going toward his car, he had Miss Leigh by the arm!"

Selznick wrote his wife a revealing account on December 12: "Myron rolled in just exactly too late, arriving about a minute and a half after the last building had fallen and burned and after the shots were completed. With him were Olivier and Vivien Leigh. Shhhh: She's the Scarlett dark horse, and looks damned good. Not for anybody's ears but your own: It's narrowed down to Paulette [Goddard], Jean Arthur, Joan Bennett, and Vivien Leigh."

"You will never guess what has happened," Leigh wrote her husband, Leigh Holman, in England, "and no one is more surprised than me—you know how I only came out for a week—well, just two days before I was supposed to leave, the people who are making Gone With the Wind *saw me and said would I make a test— so what could I do?—and so now I am working frantically hard rehearsing, and studying a Southern accent which I don't find difficult anyway. These are the final tests they are making, and there are just four of us—they seem to be very pleased with me."*

Leigh's test was the last. She performed the library confrontation with Leslie Howard and the corset-lacing scene with Hattie McDaniel. Her Scarlett's near-manic excitement contrasted vividly with the hesitant, demure coquettishness of the other contenders. "I guess we're stuck with you," George Cukor told her. It was Christmas 1938.
OVERLEAF, LEFT: *Call sheet.*
OVERLEAF, RIGHT: *Leigh, in the black hat, watches the burning of Atlanta. DOS is standing by a camera, discussing the scene with one of his crew.*

CALL SHEET

1938

DATE   TUES., DEC. 21ST

PICTURE   "GONE WITH THE WIND"   DIRECTOR   GEO. CUKOR

SET   Int. Scarlett's Room   -   Dressing Scene

LOCATION   Stage #11 - B&W - Sound - CHARGE #28-9-71-23

NAME	TIME CALLED		CHARACTER, DESC., WARDROBE
	ON SET	MAKE-UP	
Paulette Goddard	10:00 AM	8:00 AM	Scarlett - as fitted
Hattie Noel	10:00 AM	9:00 AM	Mammy - " "
Standin	9:30 AM	8:30 AM	For Miss Goddard

LATER

INT. LIBRARY - STAGE #11 - PROPOSAL SCENE

Paulette Goddard			Scarlett - as fitted
Charles Quigley	11:30 AM	10:00 AM	Rhett - " "

LATER

INT. LIBRARY - STAGE #11 - PROPOSAL SCENE

Vivien Leigh	2:00 PM	12:00 M	Scarlett - as fitted
Charles Quigley			Rhett - " "

LATER

SILENT TEST ONLY

Marcella Martin	Will Call	As fitted

CAMERAS   Ready at 9:30 AM

SOUND   Ready at 10:00 AM

ASSISTANT DIRECTOR ~~ERIC STACEY~~

CHAPTER FOUR
Production

January 25, 1939

TO: John Hay Whitney

A couple of days ago I was sick with trepidation. But as of tonight—the night before we start shooting, I am filled with confidence and certain we will have a picture that will fulfill all the publicity and will completely satisfy all the readers of the book as well.

But you are going to have to bear with me for the next couple of months. They will be the toughest I have ever known—possibly the toughest any producer has ever known in the general opinion of the whole industry. We ought to feel pleased that as small an outfit as ours is making the most important picture since sound came in—and, more astonishingly, that we have wound up with a cast that could not be improved if we had the resources of all the big studios combined.

I beg you to continue to have faith in me until the picture is finished. I must refuse to be judged until the final result is in—at which time if the picture isn't everything that everyone wants, I will not only be willing, I will be anxious to leave the whole business.

—DAVID O. SELZNICK

OPPOSITE: *Leslie Howard and Vivien Leigh film the scene in the paddock. Victor Fleming is right by the camera.*

On Thursday, January 26, 1939, at 8 A.M., principal filming officially began. There was still no finished script. The final cast had only been announced on January 13, with the American principals, Clark Gable and Hattie McDaniel, outnumbered by the English principals, Vivien Leigh, Olivia de Havilland, and Leslie Howard. Vivien Leigh was separated from her paramour, Laurence Olivier, and moved into her cottage on the studio property with a friend and secretary, Sunny Alexander. Her proximity to the action was fortunate, as she would appear in about 95 percent of the scenes.

The first scene to be filmed that day was the opening porch scene with the Tarleton boys, Fred Crane and George Reeves. It did not go well. The boys' hair was too red and too wild, Vivien Leigh's dress was all wrong, and the trio was so tense they were overacting. In the afternoon they switched to the scene in which Mammy is helping Scarlett dress for the barbecue—the scene which had clinched the role for Leigh in her screen tests—and things went a bit more smoothly. The first day of filming had yielded 1½ finished scenes out of 692, and $1.1 million had been spent on the picture so far.

George Cukor, feeling somewhat like a long-distance pilot without a flight plan, was already voicing complaints about the lack of a cohesive script. Cukor wanted at least Sidney Howard's script back, if only to have the security of some continuity. But Selznick, who had begun to establish the disturbing pattern of writing the script for the next day's shooting the night before, insisted on providing the script day to day. Not only was there no continuity for the director but there was no time for the actors to prepare. Selznick was becoming impatient with Cukor's painstaking directorial approach, which placed the layered evocation of emotions and relationships above the need to

maintain a brisk filming tempo. At Cukor's pace, the picture would be only half finished before the money ran out.

Things were not smooth when Clark Gable joined the group for the filming of the Monster Bazaar sequences. Gable, unsure of his ability to fulfill the public's expectations of Rhett Butler, had steadfastly refused to adopt an accent and was not entirely comfortable working under a director who was notorious for a preoccupation, if not an obsession, with fully developing the female star's role—sometimes at the male star's expense. Selznick would later swear that Gable never complained about the attention Cukor paid to Leigh and de Havilland. But Selznick's sensitivity to Gable, the biggest star in the movies, alerted him to the fact that all was not well.

Cukor's refusal to follow Selznick's script and speed up the pacing added weight to the argument, and Cukor was finally fired on February 13. Selznick, true to his idea of the producer's role, wanted the success or failure of *GWTW* to be on his shoulders alone.

The move forced him to shut down production at a carrying cost of $10,000 per day in order to find another director. He convinced MGM that Victor Fleming, in the final throes of the Technicolor extravaganza *The Wizard of Oz*, would be the right man for the job. For Fleming, the presence of best friend Clark Gable on the set was inducement enough. Despite the fact that he was nearly exhausted, he started meetings with Selznick on Saturday, February 18—reviewing what script existed, going over what had been filmed, and discussing the production methods. With no preconceived notions about the picture or the novel (which

he hadn't read), he could accept Selznick's concepts and be objective in a way that Cukor couldn't. It was to Fleming's advantage: Though Selznick was taken aback when Fleming reiterated Cukor's complaint about having nothing to film, he took Fleming's demands for a better script seriously. He called Ben Hecht.

Talented and fast-working (and the only scriptwriter besides Sidney Howard who wasn't attached to a major studio), Hecht at first refused. He didn't know the novel, but he did know Selznick and wanted no part of the project. Fifteen thousand dollars a week changed his mind. Selznick, Fleming, and Hecht dug out Sidney Howard's script and, in a marathon session lasting five solid days, worked closely from Howard's original treatment.

"Now, I didn't know the characters," Hecht recalled, "because the treatment doesn't contain any. It just says, 'Rhett does this, Scarlett does that.' You don't know who they are. So in order to save time, they decided that they would act out . . . each treatment, tell me what the character was, and I would listen. David took the part of Scarlett O'Hara, and of Ashley, the part of Leslie Howard, the one I kept wanting to drop out of the movie, and Vic [Fleming], who was half Indian and six-feet-two and a very fine, smiling, tough-fibered gentleman, took the part of Butler and somebody else, another girl. This was rather funny, but it began at seven o'clock every morning and kept up till two A.M., and the humor got a little vague." At the end of the week, Hecht was absolutely spent, but they had a workable script for the first half of the picture. By March 2, enough of the script was available to begin filming again, and production resumed with a retake of the porch scene, directed by Fleming.

Most of what Cukor directed remains in the picture. His careful establishment of the relationships and motivations in the story's beginning carries it through to the end. Fleming, viewed as a rank newcomer by a staff who had been on the picture with Cukor for up to three years, inherited a stack of problems. The picture itself was already over budget, behind schedule, and lifeless. To rectify the situation Fleming had to take firm control over the set. As Olivia de Havilland remembers, he had a way of saying "action" that let everybody know he meant it. He energized the cast by picking up the pace and emphasizing clarity and spectacle over nuance and subtle details.

This suited Selznick, who completed the sweep-out by dismissing the gifted cameraman Lee Garmes, who had continued to photograph *GWTW* in soft, neutral tones despite Selznick's insistence on vivid hues. Ernest Haller was brought in as a replacement. A black-and-white man who had been in the motion picture business since 1913, he had a reputation for thinking on his feet. He got over his lack of experience with color features in a hurry, filming Scarlett's entrance into Twelve Oaks for the Wilkes barbecue. "The first week on *GWTW* was one of the most harrowing in my life," he recalled. "I would look at the set and members of the cast and see automatically how they would look in black and white." With only Twelve Oaks' front door and columns placed in front of Stage 11, Haller could move the camera right behind Vivien Leigh. Jack Cosgrove would add the rest of the set with his paintbrush, fooling even Howard Dietz (MGM's head of publicity) into thinking that a full set had been built.

In March 1939, Selznick rented Busch Gardens in Pasadena for the exteriors of the barbecue scene. Fleming pushed the cast and crew, averaging about three pages of script and two minutes of finished film each day. Vivien Leigh and Olivia de Havilland began making surreptitious visits to George Cukor for coaching, and Gable started to settle into his role under Fleming's familiar direction. The star had a break on March 25, when Selznick gave him six days' leave so he could travel to Kingman, Arizona to marry Carole Lombard. In his absence, Fleming filmed Ashley's Christmas dinner, an agitated Prissy packing to evacuate Atlanta, and Scarlett climbing the stairs to go to Melanie's aid. Part of the Gettysburg List sequence was filmed upon Gable's return.

Fleming's job got harder, not easier, as the production gained momentum. His further attempts to increase the filming pace were badly hampered by the lack of script, which Selznick was still rewriting daily. Sidney Howard was coaxed back onto the set for $500 a day to work on the last portions; sorely disappointed with the film he saw, he lasted less than a month. Selznick's need to have a controlling hand in every detail of the production, his refusal (or inability) to delegate, and his lack of organization were costing a fortune. His constant changes in the sets alone required continuous overtime labor. It was clear by April that a new infusion of money was necessary.

Jock Whitney and his sister Joan Payson came through, with the Bank of America agreeing to kick in additional funds only if the Whitneys would guarantee repayment. There was now more money for expensive exterior shots, but Cosgrove's special effects had become even more crucial. Worried about Cosgrove's ability to keep pace with the filming, Selznick wrote

to Ray Klune at the end of March: "I prefer Cosgrove's work to that being done by anybody in the business but I am constantly worried about the enormous number of shots that he has to make. I am afraid he is going to be weeks or even months behind. . . . Have Hal [Kern] lay out for him just which shots are needed to complete a sequence, letting go until last those which are simply for additional beauty."

Judging from the shots Cosgrove worked on, he was able to maintain high standards even while he was in a rush. Among his accomplishments were painting in the roof of Tara and the surrounding foliage, the roof of the Armory, the ceiling of the Twelve Oaks library (as well as the mansion's entire exterior), and backgrounds for the barbecue, putting in the ceiling and sun's rays at the church hospital, making composite shots of the principal actors leaving Melanie's home to escape in the wagon, matte-painting the upper part of Tara for Scarlett's night arrival, double-printing the night escape through the fire, and doing multiple prints for the pullback shots of Scarlett against the sunset.

On April 5 and 6, the Evacuation of Atlanta scene was filmed—a complicated sequence that required choreographing down to the last detail, with six hundred extras and a roiling mass of people, animals, wagons, and explosions. The extensive preparations involved plotting Vivien Leigh's path through the hundreds of panicked evacuees ahead of time to minimize the risk of being run over. Doubles could be used during rehearsals, but not in the actual take. Despite the care taken to map out her course Leigh was almost run over by a wagon, but her hoopskirts saved her, flying up as she stopped suddenly and startling the oncoming horses away.

Production intensified with the evacuation se-

quence, taking its toll on both cast and crew. Leigh's dedication, even while enduring long separations from Olivier, was unquestioned. But as the days stretched from twelve to eighteen hours, the general morale on the set seemed to plummet. There were fewer and fewer opportunities to pause and regroup, and disorganization became the norm. The crew was on call around the clock. As Ray Klune remembered, "The biggest production challenge on *GWTW* was probably David Selznick, because David used to call me between two and three in the morning, often to find out whether or not I could change the aspect of a scene." As hard as Selznick was driving the others, he was driving himself even harder. Between writing the daily script, editing the daily production with Hal Kern, casting minor characters, and paying close attention to Cosgrove's special effects, eighteen- to twenty-hour days were his norm. "I don't think he slept much," Evelyn Keyes recalled.

Meanwhile Victor Fleming and Vivien Leigh were at odds about her role, which she gamely insisted on interpreting the way she (and George Cukor) saw fit. Fleming kept pushing Leigh to display the hard, bitchy side of Scarlett—calling her "Fiddle-dee-dee" to get her temper up, while Leigh was trying to portray Scarlett as softer and more sympathetic. To break some of the tension Selznick split the production into three units: James Fitzpatrick was sent to Georgia to get atmosphere shots for the backgrounds of titles and montages; Chester Franklin took a unit to Chico, California, to film Gerald riding across the fields of Tara and find backgrounds for the postwar devastation; and Bill Menzies and Jack Cosgrove had a unit working on the bits and pieces of film needed to connect sec-

tions of the picture, adding bridges, beginnings, and endings. But Selznick's help came too late. Fleming had been fighting mental and physical exhaustion for weeks when he had one particularly difficult day: Gable refused to cry after Scarlett fell down the stairs, and Leigh made matters worse by arguing about a direction. Fleming's nerves gave way, and he walked off the set. This time, having been made aware of Fleming's possible need for a break, Selznick was prepared. He had MGM's Sam Wood waiting to step in.

Wood began on the evening of April 29, taking over direction of the first unit. Fleming, meanwhile, nursed himself back to health. It may not have been the entreaties and apologies of Selznick, Gable, and Leigh that convinced him to hasten his recovery and return to the set, so much as Wood's prowess as pinch hitter. Though *GWTW* was Wood's first Technicolor picture (it was a first for many of the crew), he kept up the pace of filming with a workmanlike confidence. Fleming returned on the afternoon of May 17, just in time to do Scarlett's vow scene on location at Lasky Mesa, near Calabasas, California.

To make it for sunrise, Vivien Leigh and the crew had to leave Culver City at 1 A.M., summoned by a crew member who had been camping out on location in a tent, waiting for the right weather. Ray Klune, meanwhile, worked on another grand scene, Scarlett's search for Dr. Meade. Klune had called for thirteen hundred extras to report to the train station, but other productions drained the resources of the Screen Extras Guild, which could provide only six hundred. Another six hundred dummies were brought in, and Cosgrove would paint in another batch of Confederate victims at the top of the shot. The biggest problem was how to film this

multitude: Klune figured he would have to rent a crane to take the camera up and back, but the longest movie cranes had only a twenty-five-foot reach. He wrote Selznick: "We are going up approximately forty-five feet and going back at least fifty feet." A crane was required with at least a sixty-foot reach: It would have to roll about twenty feet to the right of a forty-foot flagpole.

Once the 120-ton crane was rented from a shipyard, Klune discovered that it could not be started without jerking the camera. A concrete ramp well was built to the side of the flagpole, sloped downhill, away from the action. The driver of the flatbed truck supporting the crane would simply release his brakes and roll forward, pulling the crane away from the train station in one smooth motion. Victor Fleming, Ernest Haller, and Arthur Arling rode the boom of the crane and two grips steadied it. After several rehearsals, the shot was made in one take.

Fleming still had to convince Gable to cry on cue for the scene after Scarlett's miscarriage. Carole Lombard, lending a hand, got Gable to agree to break down his masculine facade. Production moved into broiling summer, which in the days before air-conditioning made stage work next to impossible. With money running out as quickly as everyone's patience, Selznick spread the load among five units to get it done. The cast and crew rallied, finishing principal photography on June 27, 1939, five months and one day after they had begun. They had taken 125 days to finish what had been estimated would take at least 200 days of filming. Vivien Leigh left for a well-earned vacation, and the Selznick studio prepared itself for the long list of fill-ins, close-ups, retakes, montages, special effects, and the myriad other shots needed before even a rough cut could be assembled for preview.

PAGES 80–81: *In her pinned-up costume, Vivien rehearses the Walk with Gerald scene, with Thomas Mitchell, January 29, 1939. The horse had inadvertently intruded into the scene. DOS was not satisfied with the background, precipitating a reshoot at a location in Malibu. The change to the white dress would come later.*

PRECEDING PAGES: *Saturday, March 4, 1939. Victor Fleming's second day on the set: the Walk with Gerald, with Vivien in the wrong dress, in a morning shot. Film editor Hal Kern remembered how unhappy Leigh was when Fleming stepped in: "Every time that she got a day or night off she would go to George Cukor's house and he would explain the scene that she was going to do the next day." Costar de Havilland was doing the same thing.*

ABOVE: *Gable waits on the ramp for his entrance during the Barbecue filming.*

RIGHT: *Extremely rare photo of a cut segment from the Barbecue scene: Scarlett and her admirers with Rhett Butler standing nearby, on location at Busch Gardens in Pasadena. Filming took place in March 1939, directed by Fleming.*

TOP LEFT: *Hattie McDaniel, Oscar Polk, and Ben Carter rest between takes on the Twelve Oaks set. Mr. Carter as "Jeems" was cut from the final print.*

CENTER LEFT: *Another rare photo: Mammy napping with the other mammies at Twelve Oaks. This scene was cut.*

BOTTOM LEFT: *A fan girl naps between takes at Twelve Oaks. All the children in* GWTW *were tutored on the set.*

ABOVE: *Fleming goes over camera angles.* "Alicia Rhett [in the foreground] *was an amateur actress in Atlanta,*" *recalled Ann Rutherford,* "*and she had won an audition in Atlanta. . . . This young woman was so good. . . . She wasn't Scarlett O'Hara, but Selznick cast her as India Wilkes. And she was excellent.*"

OVERLEAF: *Shoes in her hand, Scarlett slips out to find Ashley Wilkes.*

LEFT: *Scarlett confronts Ashley in the library at Twelve Oaks. Leslie Howard said of his costar: "I shall never forget the first time I heard her doing her stuff. The first tests I made for Ashley in Hollywood were with another actress altogether. Just as I was coming off the floor from the test, thoroughly disheartened, I heard the most terrific Southern accent on the next set. It was the best Southern I'd heard yet—talking to the colored Mammy in the scene where she pulls up Scarlett's stay laces. I asked who it was and they told me it was an English actress, Vivien Leigh, just come over to Hollywood on a visit. She had worked up her Southern accent in about five days, but she must have stuck at it like a Trojan."*

ABOVE: *Harry Wolf, the clapper boy, with Leslie Howard and a color test strip, as Leslie reads over his lines in the Wilkes library for his tempestuous scene with Scarlett. Wilbur Kurtz noted: "Leslie Howard, who played Ashley Wilkes, never read the novel. And wouldn't read it. There's a story kind of on the lot that there was a certain part of [the book] that Selznick wanted Howard to understand perfectly. And he backed him up in the corner there of his office and said, 'Damn you, Leslie! You've got to read this!' "*

OVERLEAF, LEFT: *Choreographer Eddie Prinz rehearses Leigh and Gable for their first scene together: the Bazaar sequence. It was Gable's first day on GWTW.*

OVERLEAF, RIGHT: *Clark and Vivien rehearse their waltz scene at the Bazaar, in costume. Camera operator Art Arling remembered: "Clark wasn't that keen on waltzing, figuring he wasn't a very good dancer, and they wanted those nice swinging smooth shots that the waltz evolves into. So, the mechanical department made a device where the two people were in this sort of cage, and the camera was all hooked up to this thing. We danced the camera out through the crowd, and here Rhett and Scarlet looked like they were dancing. I think Clark thought he was quite a dancer after that."*

RIGHT: *A rare photo of a cut scene of slaves reading the Gettysburg List.*

LEFT: *Scarlett runs to greet Big Sam, Tara's former foreman, as the commandeered slaves are taken out to dig trenches. Vivien Leigh insisted on doing her own part in the crowd scenes.*

ABOVE: *Belle Watling gives water to the men—this part of this scene was cut. The number of bodies and extras needed for this scene was so excessive that Selznick resorted to dummies to fill out the crowds. "I learned through the grapevine that the union was going to try to have Selznick pay for each dummy the same amount of money that us extras got," remembered Johnny Albright, an extra. "They were going to use that money to give to some extra guy that needed to work and didn't work that particular day."*

TOP LEFT: *Ed Sullivan was on the set the day they filmed Scarlett's visit to Rhett in jail.*

TOP RIGHT: *Mrs. Florence Selznick, David Selznick's mother, visits the set of postwar Tara. Selznick kept a guest book on hand for the many visitors, including a delegation from the Netherlands.*

CENTER LEFT: *Gable, looking handsome against the sky, with newspaperman Walter Lippmann. News of production was in the papers daily.*

BOTTOM LEFT: *Director Sam Wood, who took over some scenes for Fleming in the middle of filming, on the set of Ellen's office with Leslie Howard, Vivien Leigh, and former governor of New York, Al Smith.*

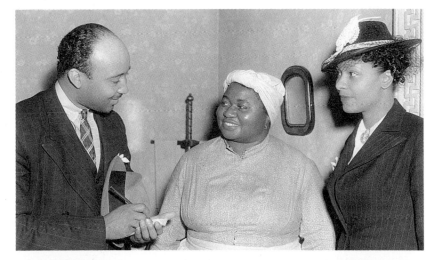

TOP LEFT: Hattie McDaniel reads Flash *magazine with Vernon Kindred, a visitor to the set. Aged with gray hair, she was in the middle of filming the birth of Bonnie.*

TOP RIGHT: Hattie McDaniel with two fans. According to Wilbur Kurtz: "There was one place where she just about stole the show. She was born in Kansas. Her grandparents had been slaves in Georgia. Selznick could hand her her part of the script and count on her to know exactly what to do with it, which she proceeded to do. She even threw in certain businesses without any direction from the script or from the director."

CENTER RIGHT: Vivien Leigh with her friend and secretary, Sunny Alexander. Selznick moved both into a cottage right on the set to whitewash Leigh's affair with Laurence Olivier.

BOTTOM RIGHT: Gable on the set with Sue Myrick and a visitor.

LEFT: Leigh, Gable, and Fleming prepare for Scarlett and Rhett's Return to Tara.

ABOVE: Selznick, Fleming, Leigh, and Gable discuss Scarlett and Rhett's final scene. "In addition to her vitality and beauty, her striking personality and enormous natural ability, Vivien Leigh had a background of training and acting that made her a fine actress," said Selznick. "Vivien made no secret of her opinion of certain scenes as she went along: During the 122 days she was on the set [of] GWTW, she groused plenty. Before a scene, she would be muttering deprecations under her breath and making small moans. According to Vivien, the situation was stupid, the dialogue silly, nobody could possibly believe the whole scene. And then, at a word from Victor Fleming, who was not merely a very fine director but a man who had the ability to conceal the iron hand in the velvet glove, she would walk into the scene and do such a magnificent job that everybody on the set would be cheering."

OVERLEAF: Extras for the Panic in Atlanta sequence have lunch on the Moorish Village set on the backlot "40 Acres." The train station can be seen in the background.

OPPOSITE: *Ona Munson poses with a gift book for still photographer Fred Parrish.*

TOP RIGHT: *February 7, 1939: Vivien Leigh and Olivia de Havilland pose in a gag version of Melanie Wilkes's labor in Atlanta. George Cukor created this scene for the benefit of Margaret Mitchell and her husband, John Marsh, who commented that Olivia's expression reminded him of the way Margaret looked when she was writing the book.*

BOTTOM RIGHT: *The real thing.*

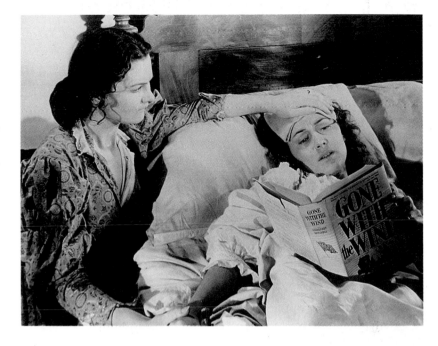

ABOVE: *Happy birthday to Olivia de Havilland—July 1, 1939.*

RIGHT: *Ashley's birthday party with some of the same guests.*

OVERLEAF, LEFT: *Scarlett and Rhett: bad dreams.*

OVERLEAF, RIGHT: *Scarlett and Ashley: Melanie's death.*

8-108-142

LEFT: *Scarlett's final walk to Tara. The scene was cut from the final print.*
OPPOSITE: *October 13, 1939. A delighted Selznick accepts Scarlett's daffodils upon completion of the final retakes of the porch scene (as directed, this time, by Victor Fleming).*

It was a happy ending for Leigh after a summer-long hiatus—which Selznick had made sure got off to a good start. As soon as she finished her final scene during GWTW's main production phase (on June 27, 1939), Selznick cabled Jock Whitney: "Scarlett O'Hàra completed her performance at noon today, Gable finishes tonight or in the morning and we will be shooting Friday with bit people. I am going on the boat Friday night and you can all go to the devil. We are trying to keep Vivien's arrival in New York Thursday a secret. Herbert will accompany her and will look you up. Vivien is expecting a call from you so if you can arrange one evening on Sunday for her and Larry I think it would be a nice thing to do."

PRECEDING PAGES, LEFT: *The Technicolor camera on its trolley is moved by a crew of 16 to shoot the Walking the Baby sequence.*

PRECEDING PAGES, RIGHT: *Leigh and Gable rehearse the scene with an empty stroller.* "Toward the end," recalled Olivia de Havilland, "when Larry [Olivier] was on Broadway playing with Katharine Cornell, Vivien would shoot all day with the rest of us and then go back after dinner and work until midnight, to finish sooner and get to New York. She gave something to that film which I don't think she ever got back."

CHAPTER FIVE
Sets

Mr. Selznick asked me, "What did Atlanta look like in 1862?" "Well," I said, "it had a population of something like ten thousand in 1860. It had a city hall of some architectural pretensions." The question I was answering was this: In what manner did Atlanta differ from any other Western town? He was thinking about the same kind of movie sets that are used in Wild West things. A city hall of architectural pretensions. Three churches with tall spires pointing heavenward. Gaslight street illumination. Three-story buildings. And a car shed built to accommodate the four railroads of Atlanta. A huge structure. . . . "You say that's the car shed that is mentioned in the novel?" "Yes sir." "Well, I thought it was one of those little butterfly sheds that you see at railroad stations today." "No," I said, "it was one hundred feet by three hundred feet long. It had four railroad tracks running through it." He slammed his fist on the table and said, "We'll build it."

—WILBUR KURTZ

OPPOSITE Lyle Wheeler with his miniature version of Atlanta, which was built with the aid of a bird's-eye-view painting by Wilbur Kurtz. OVERLEAF: Rehearsal for the scene at Twelve Oaks. De Havilland and Leigh wait for their cues.

* SELZNICK SET STILL *
DIRECTOR EASON
PIC. No 108 | SET No 45
Remarks Big Bank
EXT
Woods

Based on a novel set in a very particular time—from 1861 to 1872—and a very particular place—north Georgia—a novel which had been read by millions of devoted fans, none of whom would accept the slightest deviation in setting or character, *Gone With the Wind* was not a movie to spare its technical staff any challenges.

Selznick's insistence on historical authenticity drove him to enlist the talents of three men: William Cameron Menzies, who had worked for Selznick on *The Adventures of Tom Sawyer*, Lyle Wheeler, who had already served as an art director for Selznick at MGM, and Wilbur Kurtz, the historian from Atlanta.

Selznick hired Menzies to be *GWTW*'s production designer in the fall of 1937, long before filming had actually started. Menzies was the first to visualize *GWTW*, using both the novel and the script (when it was finally ready) to place the entire story on highly detailed, watercolor storyboards. He got around Selznick's tendency to procrastinate by working on sets for scenes that would have to be in the film—Tara, Twelve Oaks, Aunt Pittypat's house, the Monster Bazaar, and the streets of Atlanta—regardless of what else would be cut. At this point, he was working only from the novel.

Menzies had begun as an illustrator of children's books before breaking into Hollywood in the early 1920s, where he more or less invented the position of art director, winning the first Academy Award given for art direction in 1928, and he also directed several films. He was responsible for the classically exotic look of some of the best movies of Rudolph Valentino and Douglas Fairbanks, Sr. His broad experience, combined with a renowned visual acuity and talent for color, resulted in a new job description: production designer, with responsibilities reaching far beyond the art director's tasks of designing and building sets.

Selznick described Menzies as spending almost an entire year "laying out camera angles, lighting effects," and making important contributions to the film's direction, most of which "are in the picture just as he designed them a year before Vic Fleming came on." "He was an absolute genius," cameraman Arthur Fellows recalled. "I used to watch him paint, and when the paintings were finished, you could really feel what it was all about and what the final picture was going to look like. These storyboards were used by the cameraman to get his setups, composition, and lighting; the wardrobe designer used them to coordinate colors; the set decorator used them to paint his sets and make the furniture blend in . . . in fact, the whole look of the picture was pretty well dictated by Menzies' boards." The three thousand sketches Menzies drew of more than two hundred sets (which were finished by his assistant Macmillan Johnson and a staff of young artists) maintained continuity and unvarying cinematographic values throughout *GWTW*'s constantly changing times and settings. Menzies also directed about 15 percent of the footage, including war sequences, spectacle sequences, and montages. He knew the production as well as anyone.

To insure that production design would be "personally handled by one man [Menzies] who has little or nothing else to do," Lyle Wheeler was hired as *GWTW*'s art director. He turned Menzies' drawings into finished set designs and blueprints for the construction department. In effect, Wheeler, who had trained as an architect before beginning his Hollywood career in 1929, served as the architect for the ninety *GWTW* interior and exterior sets and more than fifty full-scale

buildings, using more than 1 million feet of lumber. He also constructed the quarter-inch scale models of the sets used by the director and cameraman to work out lighting schemes, by Selznick and Menzies to check design, and by Wilbur Kurtz, the production's resident historian, to verify authenticity.

Kurtz had been recommended to Selznick by Margaret Mitchell after she succeeded in convincing Selznick that she herself really didn't want the job of historical consultant. His reputation as an authority on the Civil War was certainly well founded (Mitchell depended upon his expertise to assure the historical accuracy of her book). During his tireless research he had interviewed both her father and brother among countless witnesses and history buffs. His consuming interest had always been the Civil War, although he made his living as a commercial artist, having spent five years (1904–9) at the Art Institute of Chicago in his native Illinois. What he modestly called his hobby turned out to be a boon for *GWTW*: He recorded, photographed, and painted historical sites. His watercolor bird's-eye view of Atlanta's business district in 1864, reconstructed from old maps and the memories of old-timers, was an invaluable guide for Wheeler's model of wartime Atlanta. His pictures of early Atlanta turned out to be far more useful than any of the thorough research Selznick's own department could produce.

"My record for knowing nothing about picture techniques was perfect," Kurtz said, but he became the watchdog for the film. His first three weeks at the studio were spent in the art department with Menzies, helping to establish the major features of the sets, and there he began sending a steady stream of memos and

schedules to various departments, complete with extensive lists of props, procedures, and instructions. He followed his memo on the Twelve Oaks barbecue with a fifteen-page report that included the fact that all the families in the area for a four-mile radius would be invited—about two hundred people—and then provided a breakdown of guests by age and sex (including mammies); a lengthy technical description of the barbecue pits, furnace, tables, and equipment (with diagrams); a description of the deportment of cooks and servants, and their props and costumes; and an interview with Will Hill, a man "so old he refuses to tell his age, if indeed he knows it," who had been at many such events.

At one point, worried that the art department would forsake the rustic character of Tara's backyard, Kurtz gave the chief draftsman a long lecture accompanied by a stack of photos. "They were about to build a well house like Marietta, slave quarters like a mill village. He stopped that," wrote Selznick. Usually in agreement, Kurtz and Selznick waged their fiercest battles over Tara and Twelve Oaks, which were being given the star treatment. Kurtz fought for Margaret Mitchell's concept of Tara against Selznick's insistence that it be embellished with exaggerated features—a row of trees leading to wide lawns, a long frontage, and a sweeping gravel driveway. After several months he was able to tone down Selznick and Menzies' excesses. Although still not quite Clayton Countyish, the compromise left Mitchell resigned but not too upset.

The battle over Twelve Oaks didn't go as well. George Cukor was convinced that it should be a glamorous representation of the Old South, implying a family with its roots in Virginia, the essence of a wealth and elegance that had been destroyed by the Civil War, and Selznick agreed. After Mitchell learned how grandiose it would be she refused to make any suggestions. Kurtz's only victory was convincing Menzies that Greek columns around three sides would be too much and that front columns would be sufficient. "Something of Tara might be found in Clayton County," he said, "but certainly not Twelve Oaks."

Ultimately, Kurtz's influence can be seen in every frame of the film. He chose, or helped to choose, everything from sets to landscaping to furniture, from endless numbers of props to the horses, carriages, and even the soil. The Burning of Atlanta scene, orchestrated by production manager Ray Klune so that the old sets on the backlot of "40 Acres" could double as the burning backdrop for Scarlett and Rhett's escape, was made possible by Kurtz. He converted the old sets from *King Kong, The Garden of Allah, Little Lord Fauntleroy,* and other pictures to *GWTW*'s flaming Atlanta railroad yards, building boxcars, attaching 1864 warehouse facades, and creating disorder with broken-down wagons and debris. Always accurate, he made sure to include the eighty-one freight car loads of ammunition the Confederates had abandoned on the night of September 1, which, when caught in the fire two months later, exploded with a force that smashed every window in the city.

Harold Fenton on the construction department came to Kurtz for information on lettering and planking boxcars; Ross Jackman of the special properties department used Kurtz to design the mock locomotive

TOP LEFT: *Studio brickmasons work on the front steps of the Tara set in January 1939. Constructing the various phases of Tara's exterior alone cost more than $16,000, including a landscape specialist. As Wilbur Kurtz recalled: "Those big oak trees that you saw in front started with a telephone post with a stick nailed to it, chicken wire over that, plaster over the chicken wire, bark worked in this soft plaster, and a huge limb from real trees brought and fastened to part of this pole and held from the top of the pole and out of camera angle by cables. Their leaves were green when they were put there but faded before they got through. They rectified that with a spray gun." But Kurtz, though humored by the artifice, insisted, for Margaret Mitchell's sake, on some authenticity when it came to the mansion's columns. "If I'm gonna take a bow on anything I did about this picture," he said, "it would be that I kept round columns off Tara."*

BOTTOM LEFT: *The completed Tara.*

OPPOSITE: *The broken-down Tara, with the cotton patch and burned-out slave quarters. In the background at left center is the cotton press. The set was built on Lasky Mesa.*

Swiftsure seen in the Gettysburg List sequence; Selznick used Kurtz to locate such minutiae as telegraph blanks, military orders, handbills, signs, advertisements, and broadsides; Harold Coles of the property department had Kurtz check and authorize the five hundred authentic rifles to be used by Confederate soldiers; and Arden Cripe asked Kurtz to okay the antique cigar case Rhett drops in the basket at the Monster Bazaar (Kurt recommended replating it instead of duplicating it in gold plate). For a movie of this scale, Kurtz was irreplaceable.

Many others participated in dressing *GWTW*'s sets. Hobe Erwin, the interior decorator who took part in early discussions on *GWTW* and traveled to Clayton County with George Cukor in mid-1937, was forced to pull out after delays in the start of filming began to cost his decorating firm more in lost business than he could make by staying on the picture. He never received screen credit. Erwin's replacement, Joseph B. Platt, a decorating consultant for *House and Garden* magazine, designer, illustrator, painter, and head of a large New York firm, took over in time to coordinate all the furniture, wallpapers, carpets, and color schemes. He scoured the country, accompanying Wilbur Kurtz and Selznick's in-house interior designer, Edward Boyle, to antique stores where Kurtz, who remembered being the one "who was supposed to know the difference between the French influence superimposed upon Clayton County rural establishment and the English traditions of Twelve Oaks," was only too glad to lean on Platt's expertise. Platt's design for Aunt Pittypat's parlor has been credited with causing a revival in Victorian furnishings.

Converting Culver City, California, to Atlanta required that oak trees be built out of telephone poles, chicken wire, plaster, and paint; lawns and trees be brought in; sets be aged and weathered. Making smooth roads rutted and muddy posed the problem of how to turn brown California soil into red Georgia clay. Brick dust was tried unsuccessfully. The solution was ordinary red drainage tile—pulverized and sacked up by the ton. Just before filming, "the property people would take buckets of it and scatter it on the ground," recalled Kurtz.

To find the 1,100 horses (many of which pulled the 450 wagons, ambulances, and caissons in the picture) and 375 assorted pigs, mules, oxen, cows, dogs, and turkeys required, Kurtz, Harold Coles, and William Clark (a former Arizona ranchman, stunt rider, and animal trainer in charge of livestock for SIP) canvassed the countryside farms and ranches that serviced the film industry, renting the beasts at a daily rate of 25 to 50 cents each. At Fat Jones's stable in North Hollywood, Kurtz found carriages and horses for the O'Haras, the Tarletons, Rhett, Pittypat, Belle, Mrs. Merriwether, the Meades, Frank Kennedy, and Scarlett, as well as oxen and horses for the artillery. He was impressed with the unlimited selection—from the "woebegone Marse Robert" (who pulled Rhett and Scarlett through the fire) to the Thoroughbreds used for the Southern aristocrats, and Ashley's magnificent Tennessee walker. The cost of maintaining the animals for the duration of filming, with Clark overseeing a staff of

Overleaf: Peachtree Street as it was under reconstruction after the war during Scarlett's futile visit to Rhett. Selznick had assumed the street was fictional until he came across Margaret Mitchell's childhood address.

160, was more than $75,000. But Selznick, always watchful of the condition of the sets, demanded realism and was willing to pay for it. From an estimate of $165,000 in October 1938, set prices escalated to $197,877 for building, $35,000 for lumber and materials, and $96,578 for rental and purchase of props—a total of about $330,000 exclusive of animal costs. But on examining the sets, props, and livestock of *GWTW*, one comes to the conclusion that "every common fault," as Selznick would say, seems to have been corrected. His money was well spent.

SELZNICK SET
DIRECTOR Mr C
PICT. No.
108
INT REMARKS
SCARLETT B

LEFT: *Scarlett's bedroom at Tara. "On the morning of the Twelve Oaks barbecue, the 'apple-green watered silk ball dress with its festoons of ecru lace,' which was to bring the emerald to her eyes and Ashley to her feet," recalled Joseph Platt, "is packed in a quaint flowered box on the bed. The fresh, neat room is up under the eaves of the house; thus the tall tester bed was built with a slope at the back to fill the wall" Also included was Scarlett's breakfast tray with two yams covered with butter, a pile of buckwheat cakes dripping in syrup, and a large slice of ham swimming in gravy.*

ABOVE, TOP: *Interior of the Tara hallway, prepared for Ellen's return from delivering Emmy Slattery's baby. Wilbur Kurtz transmitted Margaret Mitchell's suggestions for the interior of Tara.*

ABOVE, CENTER: *In contrast to the simple Tara was the entrance and staircase of Twelve Oaks, with the dining room to the left of the stairs. "I did not know whether to laugh or to throw up at the two staircases," Mitchell wrote to Susan Myrick on February 10, 1939. "Probably the Twelve* Oaks *hall will be worse than the one in* So Red the Rose. *People here in Atlanta got up and left the theater in herds when that hall was shown. God help me when the reporters get me after I've seen the picture."*

RIGHT: *Setting up a shot in the other half of the staircase. Victor Fleming is below, and George Reeves is watching from the bottom steps, left.*

OVERLEAF: *The Atlanta depot built full-size and to the original plans, covering 30,000 square feet.*

PRECEDING PAGES: *Harry Davenport as Dr. Meade on the car shed set. A shortage of extras necessitated using dummies. Johnny Albright, one of the 600 extras hired to do the scene, recalled, "I lay down, and pretty soon a prop man brought over a dummy and put him down alongside of me; then an assistant director came over and told me to reach underneath and said, 'You feel that rod underneath there? Well, move that, and when you do, his arm will move.' That indicated he was an injured soldier that needed some help. So, we did the scene, and that worked fine."*

OPPOSITE: *Rhett bids Scarlett farewell as she goes back to Tara.*

TOP RIGHT: *Doubles for Rhett and Scarlett on one of the Escape from Atlanta sets at the Baldwin Hills Pit. Margaret Mitchell "put in a week in the car with old maps figuring out what streets and roads and lands the wagon could have taken."*

CENTER RIGHT: *Menzies' drawing of the bridge Scarlett hides under to escape a Yankee detachment.*

BOTTOM RIGHT: *The bridge as built.*

ABOVE: *The burned-out exterior of Twelve Oaks was built in miniature, as were many scenes of Tara. After filming, the miniatures would be combined with full-size sets by special effects wizard Jack Cosgrove.*

OPPOSITE, TOP: *The graveyard at Tara, built on a soundstage. Graveyards of this type were standard on Southern plantations, as there were no public cemeteries in the countryside.*

OPPOSITE, BOTTOM: *Ellen O'Hara lying in state. Rather than worrying about Barbara O'Neil moving on-screen, Selznick paid $1,300 for the wax mold of her body. The candles at the bier would serve as more than props: They were used to suffuse the lower screen with warm light, while a bluish light was used for Ellen's face.*

LEFT: *On location on Lasky Mesa, at the west end of the San Fernando Valley, for filming the Confederate soldiers' return at the end of the war. Crews were constantly pouring red tile dust onto the road and hill. The cotton patches at Tara (to the right) had to be kept in different states of growth, so that filming could go on, no matter what time of year it was supposed to be.*

RIGHT: *A festive Belle Watling's. In 1962, Wilbur Kurtz recalled, "The Peachtree Street set was an old set worked over. All those studios have street sets built, just in case we're gonna need them sometime, and we usually do. There's a New York street with clotheslines across the street and wash hanging on them. Then there's a Western Street, sort of a Wells Fargo setup. And Selznick had an ordinary small-town street, which could be Atlanta with just a few alterations, one of which was to paint and post signs of well-known Atlanta merchants as of the 1860s. Those signs blossomed forth on windows and all over the doorways and so forth. It almost made me homesick."*

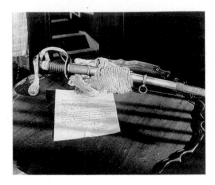

ABOVE: *Charles Hamilton's sword and the letter announcing his death in camp. "No one can conceive of the number of items needed in such work until he gets well into it," wrote Wilbur Kurtz on November 13, 1939. He did much of the meticulous lettering and handwriting of signs and texts, in addition to combing agencies for the right props. "The camera refuses to be fooled," he observed. But having expected to be ignored upon his arrival in Hollywood, he was surprised to find that Selznick directed any and all questions on Atlanta in the 1860s to him.*

RIGHT: *Scarlett in her bedroom at Aunt Pittypat's, drinking brandy out of a crystal glass.*

OVERLEAF: *"The Kiss" in front of the fussy, baubled drapery at Aunt Pittypat's Atlanta house.*

LEFT: *Scarlett and Rhett on their honeymoon at a New Orleans café. Selznick wanted the change in Scarlett's life to be unmistakable and pulled out all the stops. "Wilbur and I spent the entire afternoon on Stage 14," wrote Annie Kurtz, "where we saw another of the honeymoon scenes, the one at a fashionable New Orleans café, where Scarlett partakes of such a meal as she never could have dreamed of in those starvation days at Tara. The chef at the Ambassador Hotel himself had prepared for this scene three swans carved out of ice— these held odd candies and rare fruit. There were breasts of pheasants, doves in wine, broiled fish, all kinds of expensive cakes and pastries, liquors, and champagne. Poor Vivien! I'll bet she never ate so much before in all her life—there were many rehearsals and there could be no pretense about it—she had to eat!"*

ABOVE, TOP: *Bonnie's play area in the London hotel room.*

ABOVE, CENTER: *Bonnie Blue's deathbed. Selznick was concerned that audiences would wonder why the bed was in the middle of the room.*

ABOVE: Scarlett's dream, in which she runs down Ivy Street to find Rhett.

RIGHT: Ivy Street sidewalk by Melanie's house: Lights were projected through the slats of the fence and the branches of artificial trees to add color and drama. The trolley track for the heavy Technicolor camera ran parallel. As the camera "made an awful lot of noise," remembered GWTW's clapper boy, Harry Wolf, "they had to build a blimp to house it, and when it was in the blimp it was a little over 750 pounds."

CHAPTER SIX
Costumes

David Selznick paid attention to absolutely every detail. I don't know if people do that anymore and I think that's a loss. Do you know that he shipped in tons of red [tile] dust . . . to put on our shoes and clothes? During the Civil War we were supposed to wear the same clothes for the four years. You couldn't get new clothes and so things got dirtier and dirtier. And he brought that in. And thorns for buttons, because buttons would have been nonexistent after four years at war. Every detail!

—Evelyn Keyes

Opposite: Hattie McDaniel's change #7A: Blue-and-rose cotton print for the night of the Shantytown raid. Overleaf: Extras dress for the Atlanta Bazaar. Makeup man Monty Westmore waits to do the next step.

TOP LEFT: *Vivien Leigh in orchid percale #11.*

TOP CENTER: *Leigh in the white crepe, smocked, lace-trimmed gown used for the Rhett Leaves sequence. Leigh kept the gown, a gift from DOS.*

TOP RIGHT: *Big Sam in the tattered motley clothing worn during the evacuation of Atlanta.*

CENTER LEFT: *Thomas Mitchell in his change #1, a green tweed riding suit worn in the first scene, outside Tara.*

CENTER MIDDLE: *Leslie Howard in change #8, a suit and cape for the Shantytown raid.*

CENTER RIGHT: *Change #7A. Prince Albert suit worn for the Convict Labor scene (cost, $100).*

LEFT: *Fred Crane and George Reeves in the Tarleton twins' change #1: blue riding coats and mustard-colored britches.*

OPPOSITE: *Olivia de Havilland dressed for undressing in the Murder at Tara scene, which calls for Melanie to pull off her nightgown, give it to Scarlett, and stand there nude. "All the studio was there," recalled Walter Plunkett, "so we concocted a thing out of an old, cheap camisole, an old pair of soldier's pants, and a rope cord. . . . She did the scene very seriously with this under the nightgown the whole time."*

PICTURE No 108
WARDROBE STILL
NAME O'DE HAVILLAND
CHAR. MELANIE
CHANGE
"MURDER AT TARA"

With so much riding on the success of *Gone With the Wind*, it was to everyone's good fortune that David O. Selznick found the one costume designer who could do his masterpiece justice—Walter Plunkett. Selznick was familiar with Plunkett's passion for thorough research and period authenticity. He worked at creating costumes the way Selznick worked at creating pictures: relentlessly, creatively, exhaustively, and accurately.

Plunkett, born the same year as Selznick (1902) in Oakland, California, graduated pre-law from the University of Southern California and attended law school in Berkeley, but a consuming interest in the stage soon drew him to New York. He studied costuming while acting and dancing in vaudeville and began designing costumes for the shows. He was soon working for New York stage shows and the Metropolitan Opera, but the promise of the West Coast beckoned.

His first Hollywood role was in 1925 as a dress extra, waltzing in Eric von Stroheim's *The Merry Widow*. In 1927 he signed at FBO Pictures (later RKO) as a costume designer. Without any formal training in drawing or dressmaking, he rose to the top through determination, luck, and an innate ability to think on his feet. One piece of his luck was that David Selznick ran RKO for a period; Plunkett costumed several of Selznick's hits, including the blockbuster warm-up for *GWTW*, *King Kong*.

At RKO, Plunkett's modus operandi was to start with detailed designs and large swatches of material—found, imported, altered, or invented. Patterns had to be created by his own design department (including his own cutters and seamstresses), fittings and alterations attended to by his own tailors, black-and-white or color tests made, and costumes marked and carefully stored before he was satisfied. His techniques and their outstanding results were making him the top designer in period costuming when his patience with RKO ran out in 1935. While constantly adding to his work load, RKO

would not give Plunkett the staff and salary he required to accommodate the studio's increasing demands.

Returning to New York, Plunkett swore he would never go back to Hollywood. But he could not refuse Katharine Hepburn's urgent plea that he design her costumes for RKO's *Mary of Scotland* in 1936. When Margaret Mitchell's book came out that year Hepburn stepped in again, urging him to read it (she was vying for the part of Scarlett). Plunkett's agents, Lichtig and Englander, wrote Selznick in September; by November Plunkett was under contract to SIP. He was to research and design the wardrobes for *GWTW* for four months on a nonexclusive basis and without compensation, then receive $600 a week for at least eight weeks of preproduction work and $750 a week during production.

As soon as the ink on his contract was dry, he left for two months of costume research in the deep South, carrying Kay Brown's letters of introduction to Margaret Mitchell. Plunkett had already read Mitchell's novel three times, making extensive lists of the clothing and accessories as they'd appeared. One of his first tasks was securing Mitchell's blessing to put Scarlett in colors besides green (Mitchell's favorite). She agreed, not having realized she'd made green so prevalent and claiming she didn't care what they did with the movie anyway.

But Mitchell's efforts to help Plunkett indicated that she did indeed care about the movie. While all the people in Atlanta seemed intent on selling Plunkett their old clothes, she steered him to the sources he needed, including the women in charge of the Daughters of the Confederacy museums in Savannah and

Charleston. Plunkett rightly felt they'd give him the best information on how clothes were made inside the Union navy's blockade.

From donated samples of fabrics clipped from hems and seams, including samples of the plaids used in those days, Plunkett made countless sketches. From his work in 1933 on *Little Women* (also set in the 1860s), Plunkett was already familiar with *Godey's Ladies Book* and *Petersen's Magazine*, fashion publications from that period. He traveled extensively at his own expense: He found a textile mill near Philadelphia that still produced patterns from swatch books dating back to the 1840s, and made a deal with them to furnish the fabrics for *GWTW* and then merchandise them after the film was released. Most of the patterns were too small to photograph well: Plunkett had to double the size of the green sprigged pattern of Scarlett's silk muslin barbecue dress and then screen-print it onto the material. One pattern that did work was the lavender calico (orchid percale) worn by Scarlett through so much of the picture; since twenty-seven copies of the dress had to be made, Plunkett's mill trip turned out to be quite worthwhile.

Plunkett finished in November 1937 with a trip to Paris to research hoopskirts and bustles. He knew he would have to take the ladies' costumes through two major changes: from the hoops of prewar and wartime to the straight skirts of postwar, early Reconstruction poverty; and then to the bustles of late Reconstruction and the return, for some, to prosperity. He went back to SIP, his head overflowing with *GWTW*, but the script was not ready, and Selznick asked him to do *Nothing Sacred* in the meantime.

Later Plunkett would relate, ". . . My *GWTW* research and my *GWTW* notebooks were stacked at the end of the desk, and I was weeping while I was doing [other things]. . . . Still there was no script, so he put me onto *Tom Sawyer*. There I should have had an inkling of how completely cold-blooded David was about things. . . . And still my research sat at the end of the desk, and I kept reading and trying to think of more things for it." His contract expired and he was forced to return to RKO to make a living for the time being, but he finally got word that the script had been written. Selznick was going to start filming, and he was wanted in Hollywood.

Considering Plunkett's inspired designs for *GWTW*, especially for Scarlett, it seems strange that Selznick was still looking at sketches by other designers as late as January 1939. Selznick thought of hiring another designer to finish the movie after Plunkett's original contract ran out in August 1937. Margaret Mitchell, after seeing the designs Muriel King had made for Scarlett's costumes, preferred King's, as did George Cukor.

Similarly unexcited with Plunkett's work, Selznick stalled on signing Plunkett until he had looked thoroughly for someone less expensive. Again, Plunkett's luck held: No designer could be coaxed into working cheaply for the difficult Selznick. Even Muriel King had held out for $750 per week—just to do Scarlett's costumes. But Selznick's fear that he would have to hire another designer to do a half dozen or so "sensational" costumes (since Plunkett's work would be based purely on research) was soon allayed; he wired Kay Brown on January 6, 1939, to say that "Plunkett has come to life."

At SIP Plunkett began work immediately, hiring seamstresses experienced in period clothes to fashion the hundreds of hoops required and sending for the acres of fabric the Philadelphia mill was providing for the barbecue and other scenes. He had to complete what would amount to nearly four hundred sketches for clothing, hats, parasols, dolmans, and accessories. At least thirty-five hats were already designed, but again Selznick was looking for "something sensational" and made a deal with New York milliner John Frederics to design Scarlett's hats. Mr. John was reimbursed for transportation and living expenses; his profit came from publicity alone. "Thanks so much for the loan of the *GWTW* hats," he cabled Selznick on November 10, 1939, after Selznick had finally agreed to lend him hats that would not be needed in retakes for Mr. John's fall show. "Every store in the country wants them for when this picture comes to their town." But Mr. John received only program credit; he was never listed in the movie.

Plunkett had to swallow his pride and cooperate. The hats, made with materials the milliner claimed were available only in New York, are probably the least authentic items of clothing in *GWTW*.

The numbers surrounding the costuming of *GWTW* are staggering: Plunkett had to create 5,500 separate items of clothing and oversee a total costuming effort that cost $154,000. There were 59 major characters to design for and dress, with 206 changes for the principal women and 83 changes for the principal men. Hundreds of rented costumes (from MGM and Western Costume) had to be fitted. Thousands of extras had to be dressed and monitored, somehow, for accuracy. Crowd scenes had to be controlled to ensure that

LEFT: *Extras lace up for the Twelve Oaks Slumber scene. Selznick wanted authenticity right down to the underwear: pantaloons, petticoats, and eyelet ruffles. Plunkett went to great lengths to find the real thing. While researching in Atlanta he came across a bounty: a woman with a trunkful of underpinnings. "I arrived at the house and rang the doorbell, and there was a kind of scurrying around on the inside of the house, and I kept waiting and waiting, and finally she came out to the door and she said, 'Oh! Mr. Plunkett, I'm so sorry! When I looked out and saw you here, you were wearing a blue suit, and Mama's loose, and to Mama, any man in a blue suit is a damned Yankee, so I had to put her away!' "*

ABOVE: *A classic disappointment as Mammy measures the new mother's corseted waist in the No More Children sequence.*

LEFT: In her widow's weeds, Scarlett agrees to dance the Virginia reel with Rhett, scandalizing the Atlanta aristocracy.

TOP: The black bengaline bonnet for change #4.

CENTER: Plunkett's original sketch. The dress cost $350.

BOTTOM: Leigh is assisted by her dresser before the Bazaar sequence.

the proportion of men to women, and the percentage of those in mourning, would reflect the conditions (and casualties) of the year being filmed. As the war progressed, there had to be fewer men and more women in mourning.

For the most part Selznick encouraged Plunkett's obsession with authenticity, insisting on accuracy right down to underwear and shoes—convinced that this would help the actors with their characterizations. It took some ingenuity: To make the last twelve or so of the twenty-seven copies of Scarlett's orchid percale dress look faded, Plunkett turned them inside out. Reasoning that the O'Haras would have had insufficient time to properly tailor and shorten Ellen O'Hara's wedding dress to fit Scarlett, he had the dress made to fit Barbara O'Neil's taller figure. The gown's large sleeves—seen on no other costume—can be traced back to the fashion of 1844, when Ellen married Gerald O'Hara. Though Scarlett's wedding gown started a fad among brides, probably few realized what they were imitating.

Plunkett had more trouble satisfactorily costuming Clark Gable, the biggest star (male or female) in the world at that time. Plunkett's tailor had designed Gable's costumes so that they looked perfect only when he stood perfectly straight. Gable was also miffed because his own trusted tailor, Eddie Schmidt, had been refused him. Gable wouldn't cooperate with the costuming process as he had in the past until Selznick ordered Eddie Schmidt brought in.

Selznick did join forces with Plunkett when he felt their production values were threatened by the interference of the Technicolor consultant, Natalie Kalmus. She had veto power over any color combina-tion that might be inappropriate to the Technicolor process, including the right to toss out costumes. Selznick objected strenuously to Kalmus's domination of Plunkett's choices: She was forbidding bright, rich colors and replacing them with soft hues and pastels. Selznick felt that the Technicolor advisers should be there to guide, not dominate, and Plunkett won the right to use his vivid color schemes. For the first third of the picture, the costumes are bright and rich. For the middle the colors are neutral, reflecting poverty and sadness. The final third of the picture contrasts the two schemes: Scarlett's gaudy finery is shown next to the somber hues of her still-impoverished neighbors.

Plunkett established the definitive archetype of the Civil War-era Southern belle with his costuming for Scarlett O'Hara, even if he bowed slightly to the fashions of his day. Fashion historian Edward Maeder noted, "Audiences were dazzled by Scarlett's barbecue dress. . . . Viewers left the theater convinced they had just seen a true reflection of the past; but . . . a fashion historian cannot help noticing that many of the film's costumes' styles are rooted more in the 1930s than in the 1860s. In all the dresses for the film, bodices were cut to conform to the shape of the bosom; in the 1860s the bosom conformed to the corset. The crinolines in the film are exaggerated. . . . Even the men's suits in the picture reflect the late-1930s cut."

Although there was no Oscar for costume design in 1940, Plunkett became known in the industry as its finest designer—especially for period films. Plunkett's attention to detail, control, and accuracy was Selznick's system in microcosm. He placed costuming on a level with scripting and directing: No effort was spared, no obstruction tolerated.

OPPOSITE: *Back at Tara, the orchid per-cale, its hem in tatters, badly soiled from the traumatic flight out of Atlanta, became, in the words of Wilbur Kurtz, "a suit of armor for the embattled Scarlett." The dress was one of Plunkett's earliest decisions, as Leigh's double would have to wear it first during the Fire scene, which appeared mid-way in the movie. From a print manufac-tured at the Pennsylvania mill, Plunkett made 27 separate, identical dresses, all as-signed numbers and kept in careful order on their own rack. Five were used for doubles in the beginning alone; dress #1 was pre-served for retakes.*

ABOVE: *The last appearance of the dress as Scarlett goes for the green velvet portieres, scheming how she'll appeal to Rhett. If one of the versions of the dress was torn, burned, or bleached during a scene, ward-robe would tear, burn, or bleach the others exactly the same way. Getting the dress to fade for its last appearances was a problem. Plunkett remembered, "We couldn't bleach any further. The dye was just too strong. . . . So, the last 5 or 6 were ripped apart and turned inside out because the color was weaker on the wrong side."*

OPPOSITE: *Plunkett followed Margaret Mitchell's preference for green when he made Scarlett's change #16 for the visit to Rhett in jail. The green velvet drapery dress has a sash cord belt and cock's-feather hat (2 were made). The material was faded slightly to show the effects of constant sunlight. Total cost: $400 for the dress; $85 for the hats.*

ABOVE LEFT: *Leigh in one of Scarlett's gaudiest changes, #22, a white bengaline dress with black trim and a white bonnet with black veil. Worn in the New Orleans living room after Scarlett's shopping spree, it was intended to show her garish response to newfound affluence. Wilbur Kurtz called it one of the creations "that would make a Parisian couturier retire to a cave for fasting and prayer."*

ABOVE RIGHT: *Scarlett's change #9: white satin, shirred blouse, maroon taffeta skirt. A more demure outfit for the Yellow Sash sequence at Aunt Pittypat's house, earlier in the movie.*

OVERLEAF, LEFT: *Plunkett admiring Ona Munson in Belle Watling's change #2, a red satin skirt and red velvet jacket worn for her visit to the jailed Rhett.*

OVERLEAF, RIGHT: *De Havilland hams it up for a mock publicity shot as Plunkett pins the hem of her patched-together skirt, part blue plaid wool from one of Carreen O'Hara's old outfits, and part black taffeta from a dress of Ellen O'Hara's. Worn with an old white cotton blouse and a burlap shawl, change #9 was appropriate for a Melanie who had fled to Tara in only her nightgown; it is worn in many scenes after the war.*

FOLLOWING PAGES, LEFT: *Belle Watling's change #3: yellow satin with black petal lace and a bell headdress, worn for Rhett's visit to her house (cost, $350).*

FOLLOWING PAGES, RIGHT: *Melanie Wilkes's change #2, worn for Scarlett's marriage to Charles Hamilton: a blue taffeta dress, lace trimmed, costing $350.*

LEFT: *The O'Hara family. Thomas Mitchell in rumpled finery, Leigh in the white dress, Barbara O'Neil in stately black taffeta with velvet trim, Ann Rutherford in Carreen's blue plaid (cut up in the story to make a skirt for Melanie), and Evelyn Keyes in Suellen's yellow-dotted organdy with brown velvet trim, which features Plunkett's trademark chevron design.*

BELOW: *Butterfly McQueen assisted by her dresser for filming. Plunkett kept the characters in mind while designing: Prissy's brown homespun dress is trimmed at the shoulders with cast-off baubles.*

S.I.P-108_5

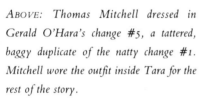

ABOVE: Thomas Mitchell dressed in Gerald O'Hara's change #5, a tattered, baggy duplicate of the natty change #1. Mitchell wore the outfit inside Tara for the rest of the story.

ABOVE: Victor Jory as Jonas Wilkerson, dressed in his carpetbagger's clothes: a green stripe coat and gray trousers.

ABOVE: Suit and vest worn by Ernest Whitman as Jonas Wilkerson's carpetbagging friend during the Returning Soldiers scene. OPPOSITE: A pipe-smoking Leslie Howard in change #3, the Confederate major's butternut uniform, hat, overcoat, and boots with spurs that Ashley wears to come home for Christmas (price, $150). Sitting behind him are some of the many women extras that were dressed in black, mourning for the loved ones that had already been killed in the war.

"Yesterday I put on my Confederate uniform for the first time," Howard said in January 1939, "and looked like a fairy doorman at the Beverly Wilshire—a fine thing at my age." Wilbur Kurtz helped with the wardrobe details—how to draw the sword and pin the Confederate medals. His input was indispensable, even with minor characters: "In nearly every instance where the coachman or carriage driver appeared, he was clad in what might have been the cast-off frippery of his master— and he always knew when or when not to wear his tall hat—and he never left the carriage box without taking his whip along."

ABOVE: *Gable relaxes in the white linen Prince Albert suit worn for the New Orleans honeymoon, surrounded by some of the results of Scarlett's shopping bonanza. Gable included the costume flop Parnell among the many reasons he was reluctant to play Rhett Butler, and felt uncomfortable in the badly fitted clothes Plunkett ordered for him from Oviatt's for the first half of the movie. Selznick sent a furious memo to wardrobe master Edward Lambert on April 17, 1939. "A more ill-fitting and unbecoming group of suits I have never seen on a laboring man, much less a star." Gable's own tailor was reinstated immediately.*

RIGHT: *An elegant prisoner plays poker with his captors in change #7: dark blue cape, dress shirt, and suit pants.*

OVERLEAF: *Tattered uniforms, shredded trousers, and dirty bandages rubbed with red tile dust: extras on location in Lasky Mesa for the soldiers' return.*

CHAPTER SEVEN
Makeup

T he Technicolor cameras made me break one tradition of a lifetime. I had to wear makeup for the first time on the screen. My own hair photographed reddish-brown in Technicolor and Ashley, as you know, was definitely "tow-headed." So, I had my hair bleached and had to use a grayish-white makeup on my face to get a natural pale skin tone.

—-Leslie Howard

Opposite and overleaf: Two views of Scarlett with her hair down for the final sequence, Walk to Tara. This scene was cut from the final edit, although the dress was used in the final pullback shot of Scarlett silhouetted against the panorama of Tara.

MAKE-UP STILL

PICTURE No 7/08

NAME SCARLETT

CHARACTER

NOTES:

The Golden Age of Hollywood (1931–40) ushered in both the heyday of the costume epic—a fantasy escape for a country burdened by the Depression—and the flourishing of the major studios, each with its own stable of glamorous stars. The studios demanded that their stars' glamorous public images—always the most contemporary—be maintained at almost any cost, which was in direct conflict with the studios' penchant for period movies. So Hollywood developed a set of rules, dubbed "the Formula" by film historian Alicia Annas: a systematic approach to makeup and hair that combined modern images with the illusion of historical accuracy.

By the late 1930s the Formula was virtually writ in stone: Sets and furnishings were almost always authentic; clothing was usually, or at least occasionally, accurate; hairstyles were correct once in a while, usually for a specific male character, such as Abe Lincoln; and no effort at all was made to effect historically accurate makeup. According to the Formula, the men in period movies wore the least bit of makeup required to meet the temperamental demands of film, to regularize their features, and to emphasize the power of the actors' eyes. They were made up to look like they weren't made up. But the women in period movies wore the same glamour makeup they did in modern films: Nothing whatsoever was done to cater to realism, and the studios and stars held firm against concessions. Movie audiences never questioned the historical inaccuracies, perhaps willing to accept the deft manipulation of craftsmen who conspired to interweave images of the past and present.

Screen makeup had originated for a much simpler purpose: to tone down actors' features (which were overemphasized by film) and to keep the actors' appearances consistent. Film tends to accentuate flaws in both faces and hair, and this was exacerbated by the silent movies' harsh arc lighting. Orthochromatic film translated all colors except red into appropriate shades of gray; red (including blood vessels in the face) became black.

TOP: *An exhausted, disheveled Scarlett returns to Tara.*

CENTER: *Hair and makeup for the I'll Never Be Hungry Again! scene, with carefully applied tear stains and hands dirty from digging in the garden.*

RIGHT: *Pale and gaunt, hair piled into a plain hair net, Scarlett decides to make a dress. Leigh's request to be made up in her dressing room was roundly denied. An exhausted Ray Klune had just finished installing the new fluorescent lighting required for Technicolor in the makeup department. "I would appreciate it if you would ask her to go to the department to be made up, just as do Miss de Havilland and the other principal women," he wrote to Selznick in a memo on January 25, 1938.*

Only heavy applications of theatrical makeup could prevent faces from photographing dark, but this obscured features, details, and even movement.

Then Max Factor, a theatrical cosmetician and wigmaker who had worked for Czar Nicholas II of Russia, invented flexible greasepaint in 1914, finally enabling moviemakers to achieve a somewhat realistic look. The cream worked with the harsh lights and film, masking the reds of the skin but allowing subtleties to show through.

The talkies of the 1920s created new problems: With sound, the noise of the arc lights was intolerable. The tungsten lights brought in, while quieter, were also softer, so moviemakers turned to panchromatic film because it was more responsive to the dimmer lights. Factor came up with Pancro, a line of makeup in a neutral spectrum that could be used in small amounts to achieve subtle shading effects. Heat-resistant, it reflected tungsten lighting properly. The result was more realistic than ever.

The introduction into use of three-strip Technicolor in the mid-1930s introduced a whole new set of variables: film so sensitive that it picked up colors from the set and costumes that were reflected in the greasepaint on the actors' faces. An actor standing opposite someone in a blue dress would photograph with a blue face; even powder could not solve the problem. Max Factor again came to the rescue with Pan-Cake, which was not grease-based or shiny and could be removed with water. By 1938 it had a place in the kits of most of Hollywood's makeup artists.

Though many silent film actors who had moved directly from stage to screen were used to applying their own makeup, professional cosmeticians were the only ones with sufficient knowledge and skill to blend the new makeup, new lighting, new film, and skin colors. During the 1930s every studio established a makeup department staffed with experts in the latest techniques, though this had as much to do with Hollywood's "star system" as with the complexities of the latest cosmetics.

Hairstyles were not as strictly bound to contemporary glamour. Most of the hairstyles in Golden Age films—whether period or not—were wigs (including hairpieces, falls, and switches), which were mounted on customized wooden heads the exact shape and dimensions of the stars' for styling by a makeup department's hairstyling staff. This saved both time and money: Studios could film sequences out of chronological order, and stars could appear in scenes requiring several hairstyles in one day. Again, there to help Hollywood was none other than Max Factor.

Max Factor and Company, renowned for the quality of their wigs, enjoyed a virtual monopoly on Hollywood wigmaking. They established an unrivaled photo archive of period hairstyles and were able to re-create any hairstyle from any period in varying degrees of historical accuracy. Producers had several alternatives: for men, complete historical accuracy; a mixture of period and contemporary (usually a contemporary hairline with period sides and back); additional facial hair to help "date" modern hair; and pure glamour, with no historical elements. For women, hairstyles often worked to bridge the gap between modern makeup and a period costume and setting: A wig with identifiable historical features would be

MAKE-UP STILL
G.W.T.W. M. WESTMORE

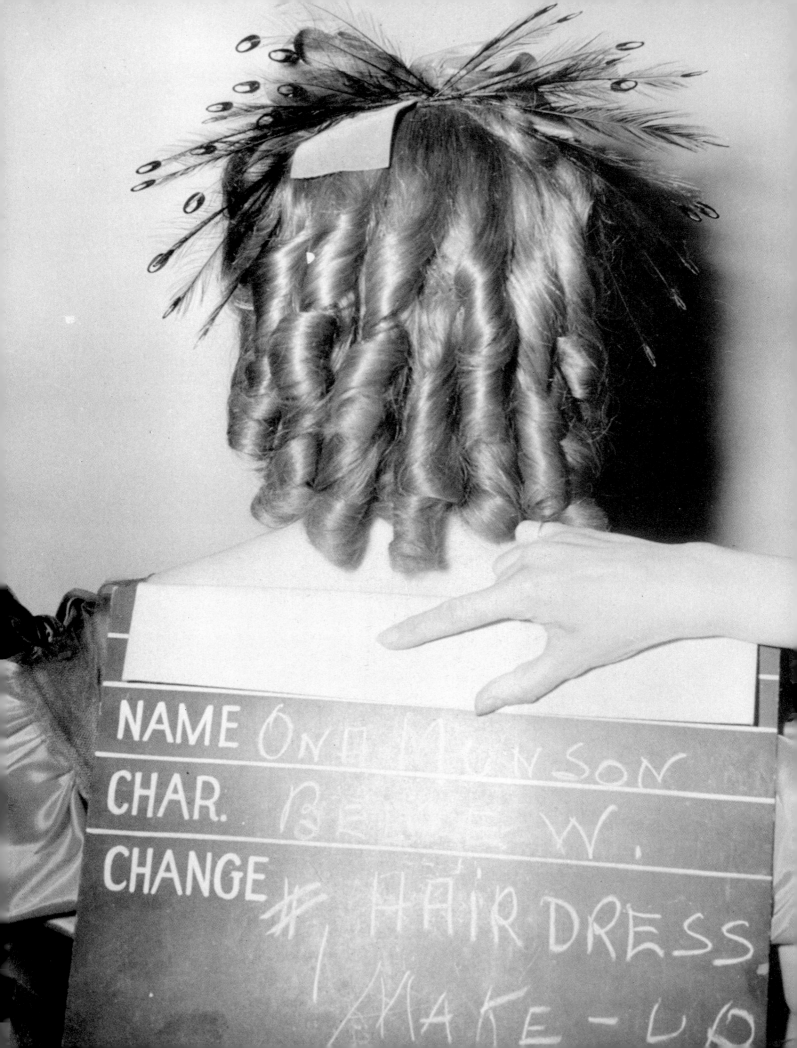

NAME One Munson
CHAR. BETTY W.
CHANGE #1 HAIRDRESS / MAKE-UP

softened and altered toward contemporary fashion; exotic styling touches would be added to suggest another time; or the image would be kept purely glamorous, though this was rare.

Even *GWTW*, frequently held up as a paragon of accuracy, gave in to the Formula to some extent. "From the first costume sketches for Rhett Butler to his final moments in the film," notes Alicia Annas, "Clark Gable's star image was not altered. The length, style, and grooming of his hair was pure Formula. His only concession to historical style was a pair of sideburns."

That the hairstyling and makeup of *GWTW* is far more accurate than in most period pictures is due to the efforts of both Selznick and Monty Westmore, the head of SIP's makeup department. Selznick, always a bit of an iconoclast, was producing three movies in 1939 that he felt required minimally made-up leading ladies: *GWTW* because of its era, *Intermezzo* because the natural look was part of Ingrid Bergman's image, and *Rebecca* because Joan Fontaine was portraying a plain woman. Choosing Monty Westmore to challenge Hollywood's glamour credo is a bit ironic: Westmore, ultimately famed for the natural appearances he created in these movies, is from a family that helped invent the movie-star look.

Among founding father George Westmore and his six sons (called the "Marrying Westmores" because the six men managed to marry eighteen women among them), one Westmore or another has managed the makeup departments for Eagle-Lion, First National, Paramount, RKO, Selznick International, 20th Century Fox, Triangle, and sundry others. They also oper-

ated the House of Westmore on Sunset Boulevard for thirty years. George Westmore, born in 1879 on England's Isle of Wight, served as a baker and barber in the army and opened a "Hair-dressing Saloon" on his return in 1901. He also married Ada Savage; Monty, his firstborn, arrived in 1902.

George moved from city to city as better opportunities arose. In Cleveland he practiced his makeup techniques on the local prostitutes, who in 1913 were the only other women besides actresses to use makeup. He also went to the movies, where his practiced eye saw how inexpertly the actors' and actresses' wigs were made and how improperly their makeup was applied. So in 1917 he packed up his family and took his skills to Hollywood, worked at a local salon, Maison Cesare, and talked his way into a job at the Selig Studio, where he established Hollywood's first makeup department. His big break came when he fashioned a new wig overnight for Billie Burke—one far better than what he was replacing. The actress was so pleased she had him revamp her entire makeup, and the change was so remarkable it landed him a job at Triangle Studios.

Monty, an independent perfectionist who found he could not get along with his father, was the first to leave home. In 1921, at age nineteen, he took a job clearing tables in the commissary of the Famous Players-Lasky Studio, during the filming of *The Sheik*. There he insinuated himself into Rudolf Valentino's confidence by volunteering to exercise his horses, posing as a horse lover distressed by the animals' lack of activity. Valentino took him on as his valet and agreed to let Monty have a try at his makeup, which Valentino

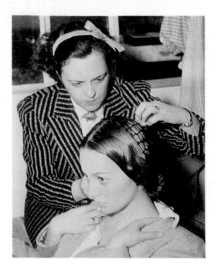

RIGHT: *Hairstylist Hazel Rogers works on Olivia de Havilland.*
OPPOSITE: *The finished product from the side. Melanie's hair swept up into a net, curled under, and fastened with an elegant comb for Ashley's birthday party. "Would you please watch on Miss Leigh and Miss*

de Havilland—the passing of time in connection with the chart that I have sent you so that we are sure to get the gradual aging as we go throughout the picture," Selznick wrote to Monty Westmore on February 8, 1939.

had been doing himself. Monty cleaned up his hair, made him up to emphasize his sensuality, and was promptly hired by the overjoyed studio bosses. He remained Valentino's makeup artist through the actor's funeral in 1926.

Working with Cecil B. DeMille on *The King of Kings* for a handsome $250 per week, Westmore started freelancing—either doing makeup for an entire movie or making stars up at their homes before they left for the studios. In 1935, Monty was doing the makeup for *Mutiny on the Bounty*, starting Clark Gable, and his work was much admired by David Selznick at MGM. Selznick managed to convince Monty to abandon his freelancing and work full-time at SIP as head of its makeup department in 1938. He soon found he had little time to devote to the House of Westmore, and, further, that the match with Selznick was not one made in heaven.

By the time *GWTW*'s filming actually began, Monty had been working on the movie for almost a year: doing research, making up actors and actresses for tests, and working on the filmed makeup tests. He was also working on *Intermezzo* and *Rebecca* and contending with the nightly stacks of studio paperwork Selznick required of his department heads. Monty's younger brother Frank, who was living with him at the time, said that he always looked ill and exhausted while working on *GWTW*, "struggling to keep up with the hyperkinetic Selznick and struggling to be a husband and father."

The struggles were intensified by Selznick's interferences; he generated an unceasing flow of memos and phone calls that went on into the wee hours of the

morning. Westmore's skill at aging people was famous, yet Selznick sent memos reminding him of the simplest concepts, like making the aging gradual throughout the film, or making sure the makeup on retakes matched that of the original takes. Both Selznick and Westmore were strict perfectionists, but with very different personalities: Selznick was articulate but insensitive; Monty was inarticulate but sensitive. He could never learn to ignore the calls and memos as others (including Alfred Hitchcock) were known to do. Instead, he spent precious time and energy going over Selznick's exaggerated and usually unreasonable missives, which blamed Monty for problems beyond his control, and tried to figure out careful responses.

Despite the interference Westmore's work was outstanding. He oversaw forty assistants and an entire department. He did all the Scarlett O'Hara screen tests. He found a way to keep Vivien Leigh's eyes looking green, as Selznick demanded, by using green eye shadow and working with the costume department to find colors that would enhance the green tints in Leigh's naturally blue eyes. Selznick never figured out how Monty pulled it off.

Finding a compromise between the natural look and the glamorous look was nerve-racking for both Selznick and Westmore. Selznick constantly ragged Monty about the amount of makeup being used. "If you don't think Miss Leigh's mouth is made up in such a way as for it to be obvious that it *is* made up, which is of course bad for the picture, I suggest you look at the color stills, which clearly show the fantastic amount of lipstick we are using and the inexpert way in which we are using it, in that its use is

MAKE-UP STILL
PICTURE NO 108
NAME DeHAVILAND
CHARACTER MELANIE
NOTES: HAIR DRESS
PARTY

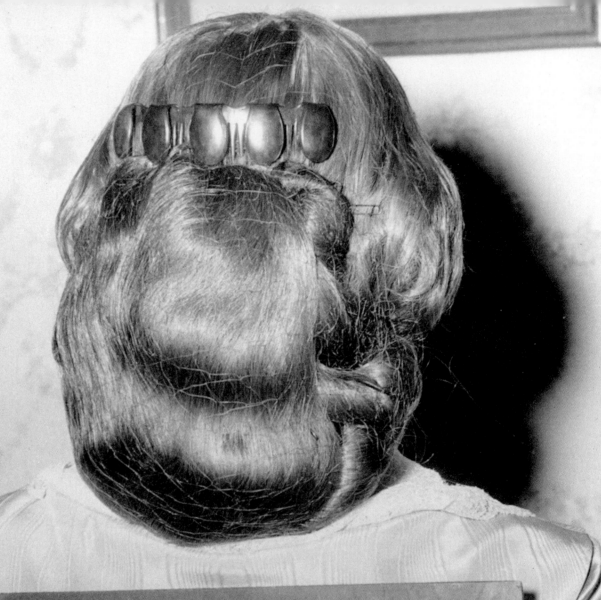

obvious," Selznick wrote to Westmore on March 11, 1939.

Although Selznick made a fetish of period research and authenticity, he was still under the sway of the glamour system. This extended to hairstyling and costumes: He briefly imported Sidney Guilaroff to do Vivien Leigh's hair as he felt Hazel Rogers's styles weren't spectacular enough; eventually, though, Rogers was reinstated to finish the film.

Aging characters of different races through the twelve-year span of *GWTW*, weathering and wounding soldiers, and marking the differences between rich and poor posed significant makeup challenges for Westmore. The problems in makeup were roughly paralleled in hairstyling: Selznick's research department had unearthed tintypes and daguerreotypes of period hairstyles authenticated by Susan Myrick (*GWTW*'s technical consultant) for Westmore to consult when creating the hairstyles for the cast, and Monty followed Selznick's strictures on authenticity for the vast majority. The hairstyles were duplicates of the styles of the 1860–70 period. But when it came to the stars, the strictures were loosened: Exceptions to

the rules on period grooming were condoned, if not encouraged. Here again, Selznick's upbringing in the studio system was in evidence: Slight deviations from historical accuracy were permitted for the sake of correct star image.

Even struggles with three difficult movies, a demanding producer, constantly changing job requirements, a large department, and a salon could not dampen Monty's spirit. He had an irrepressible sense of humor, and the salty tongue of a seaman, which he used to embellish his tales of the stars and their foibles (he had no respect for actors). He thoroughly enjoyed regaling the crew and technicians with embarrassingly intimate details of the stars' private lives that only he could have known. In the end, perhaps, the industry struck back: Soon after a tonsillectomy in April 1940, he suffered a fatal heart attack. He was thirty-eight. His doctor, William Branch, blamed the horrendous work load and stress of Monty's previous two years, which, despite his dedication, did not even earn him screen credit for *Gone With the Wind*, as makeup artists, by industry custom, did not receive screen credit until the early 1940s.

MAKE-UP STILL

PICTURE No 108

NAME MISS CREWS

CHARACTER Pitty

NOTES: HAIR DRESS PARTY

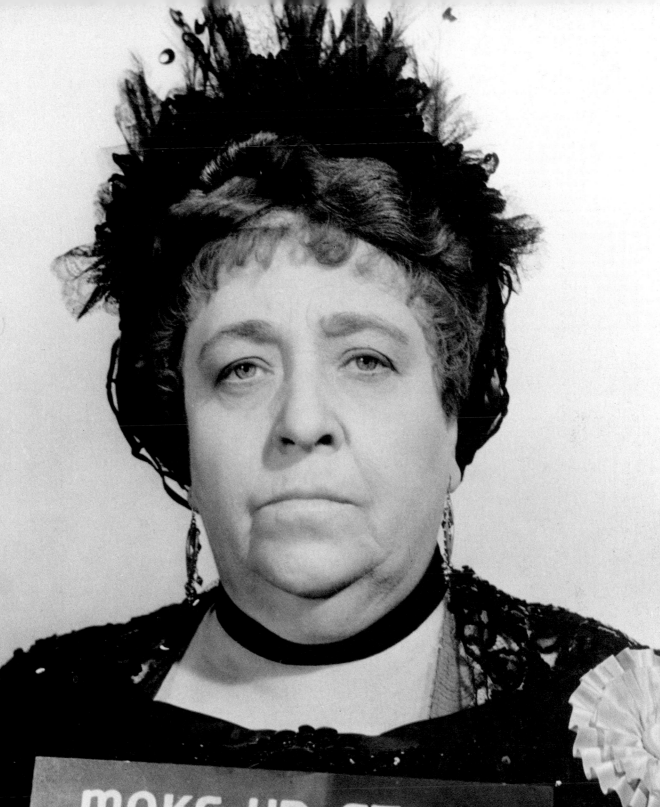

MAKE-UP STILL
PICTURE № 108
NAME J. DARWELL
CHARACTER MERRI WEATH
NOTES:

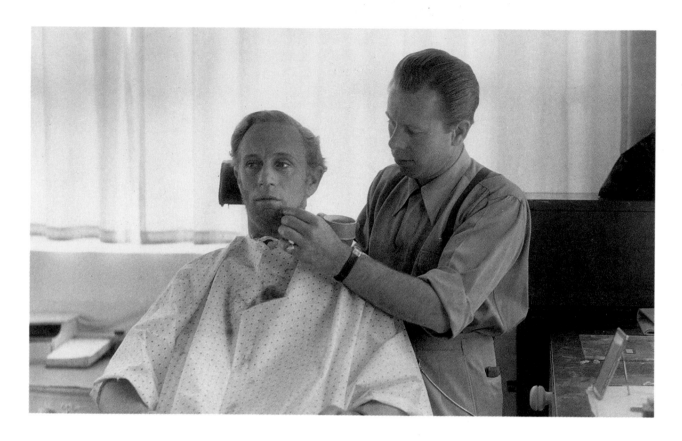

ABOVE: *Monty Westmore applies a week's growth of beard on Leslie Howard for Ashley's return from a Northern prison. The stubble was applied right over the makeup.*

OPPOSITE: *A weary Ashley Wilkes returns to Tara after the war, sporting a hand-applied beard.*

MAKE-UP STILL
PICTURE Nº WIND
NAME CARROLL NYE
CHARACTER FRANK KENNEDY
NOTES:

OPPOSITE: *Carroll Nye made up as the young Frank Kennedy, who appeared at the Wilkes barbecue, about to embark on a remarkable aging process.*

ABOVE: *Nye and Westmore hold the portrait of Jefferson Davis that Westmore used as a model for Frank Kennedy as a storekeeper, just before his death during the Shantytown raid.*

LEFT: *Westmore combs Nye's new beard. Studio notes included this one: "Time lapse is 2 or 3 years to hospital—but he should look horribly tired as if he's been through hell. Time lapse of 3 or 4 years to later scene in Atlanta, but should take the liberty of making him 10 years older between the first and last appearance. There should be not simply a difference in years—but he should show signs of suffering and hardship."*

OVERLEAF, LEFT: *Frank Kennedy as he returned from the war.*

OVERLEAF, RIGHT: *Paul Hurst as the battle-scarred renegade cavalryman who meets his end at the point of Scarlett's revolver.*

MAKE-UP STILL
PICTURE No. 108
NAME CAROL NYE
CHARACTER E, KENNEN
NOTES:

SELZNICK MAKE-UP STILL
PLAYER *PAUL HURST*
HAR. *Yankee Calvaryman*
TES

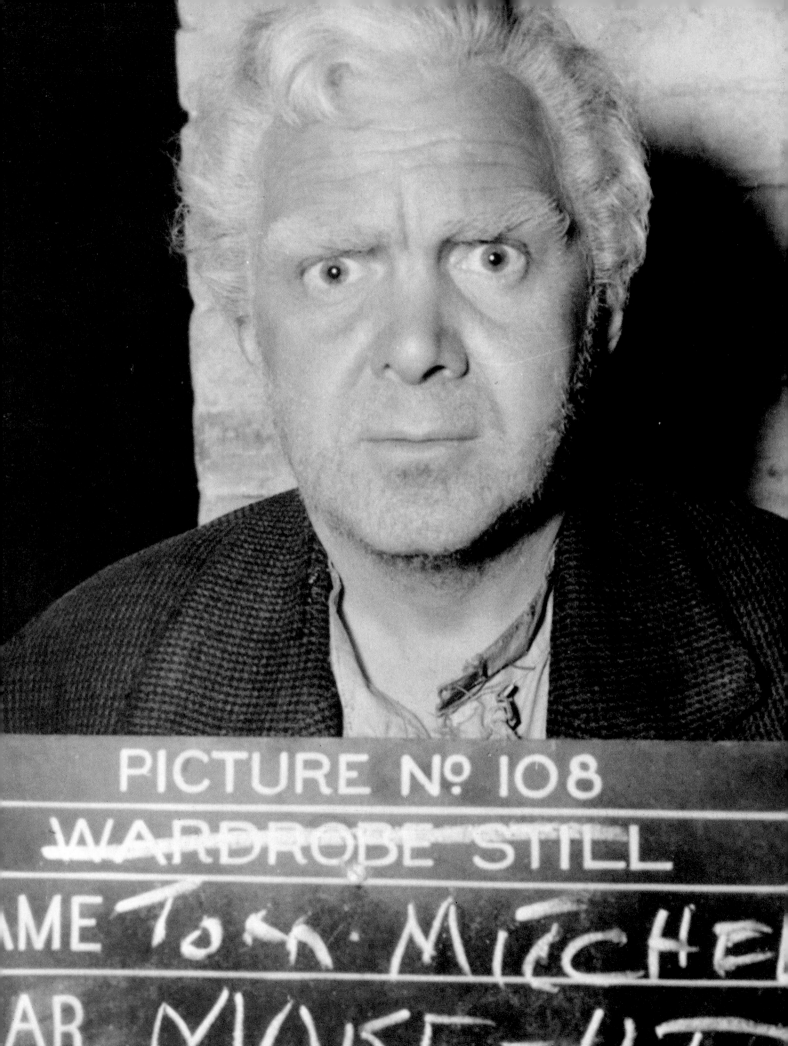

PICTURE Nº 108

WARDROBE STILL

AME TOM MITCHE

AR MOSE-HT

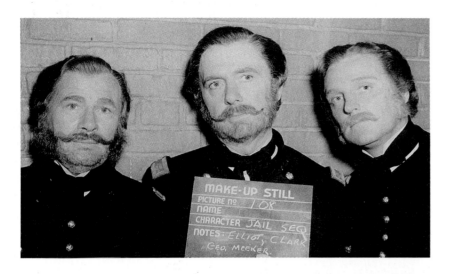

Opposite: Gerald O'Hara, haunted by Ellen's death, his hair and eyebrows gone gray.

Above left: Robert Elliott, Wallis Clark, and George Meeker as Rhett Butler's poker partners in the Atlanta jail, complete with waxed mustaches. Special care was taken to make the extras and bit players look realistic.

Above right: Howard Hickman as John Wilkes, Ashley's father, as he appeared when Scarlett found him dying in the hospital. The scene was cut.

Right: Robert Gleckler as the evil Jonas Wilkerson. Victor Jory took over the part upon Gleckler's untimely death.

Far right: Ward Bond as the Confederate Captain Tom.

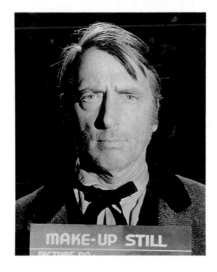

CHAPTER EIGHT
Postproduction

Here we were after more than three years. . . . It was the longest running emergency on record. David was afraid we were being followed; I was worried as we passed town after town that it would get too late. We finally pulled up at the theater in Riverside and David, standing on the pavement, signaled the manager. As David introduced himself the manager obviously jumped to the right conclusion because he threw out his arms promising anything . . . anything!

—IRENE SELZNICK,

ON THE DRIVE TO THE SNEAK PREVIEW

OPPOSITE: *Page from Max Steiner's score, including the immortal "Tara" theme.*

ABOVE: *The editing room at SIP. Hal Kern is holding up the 35 mm film, center. Viewing machine is on the left, splicer on the right.*

LEFT: *Special effects whiz Jack Cosgrove.*

ABOVE: *Austrian-born Max Steiner, whose score for GWTW was the longest ever written. He composed it in just 16 weeks, from August 14 to December 5, 1939, just 10 days before the Atlanta première, by working, from 5 A.M. to midnight every day, sustained by injections of vitamins. He was also responsible for scoring two other pictures, including Selznick's Intermezzo, during this same period.*

Training at Vienna's Imperial Academy of Music (he completed the four-year program in one year) gave Steiner a first-rate background to score films. One of his first jobs was one reel of music for RKO's Symphony of Six Million, produced by Selznick, *who was so impressed with the one reel that he had Steiner score the rest of the film. A year later, Merian Cooper gave Steiner his big break with* King Kong: *Steiner had carte blanche and hired an 80-piece orchestra, ringing up a $50,000 bill.*

All told, Steiner wrote 168 scores between 1929 and 1939, including 12 in 1939, and would write 138 more before retiring in 1965. For Gone With the Wind *he weaved folk tunes, military pieces, and patriotic songs through 3 hours and 45 minutes of original music. Divided in 282 separate musical segments, the score includes 16 major themes (including Mammy's, Scarlett's, Gerald O'Hara's, and Melanie's).*

Within a week after filming ended, Selznick's editor Hal Kern and associate editor Jim Newcom had a rough cut assembled that was six hours long. With the aim of previewing the film in eight weeks, the three men spent July in marathon editing sessions, trying to pare the picture down to five hours, putting in temporary music tracks at the same time. Work went on day and night, beginning at 9 A.M., with an hour break for dinner twelve hours later, and resuming upon Selznick's return until 1 or 2 A.M. "Sometimes he gambled a little and didn't get back quite as soon," recalled Newcom. For efficiency, the sections that had just been edited would be reviewed the same night.

Selznick placed great stock in the ability of editing to improve a picture. Reducing the scope of the train yard fire not only saved time but also put the fire scene in its proper perspective, making it plain that only the depot was burning. As the movie began to take shape in the cutting room, Selznick decided it deserved titles as grand as it would be. Hal Kern tried titles in which each letter of the words *Gone With the Wind* filled the screen. But the effect was lost. What finally worked was painting each word on individual plate-glass sheets and having three men roll each sheet in front of the camera on a dolly. It is still the biggest title ever made to date.

By September 9, 1939, a previewable picture was finally ready. It was still rough at 4½ hours long, with Wilbur Kurtz paintings for titles, and had a sound track borrowed from *The Prisoner of Zenda* and other MGM pictures. By now, with the making of the film a national obsession, the press and public were impatient, and plans for the preview had to be shrouded in secrecy. Hal Kern, David and Irene Selznick, Bobby Keon (the production secretary), and Jock Whitney took off from the Selznick house in two cars, cans of film in hand, in the late afternoon, heading toward Riverside. It was an anxious drive, recalled Irene Selznick:

> The heat was searing and the further we went the hotter it became. There was either a dead sound or we were all talking at once. We couldn't sit back properly in the car. . . . One or the other of us was always inching forward and so reminded and then pulling back. Eventually we all realized that the three of us were sitting on the very edge of the seat . . . that was the only laugh we had on the way out.

After they had picked a theater, they had its elated manager cut off the show, announce a very long sneak preview, and tell the audience that after a five-minute intermission the doors would be locked: Anyone could leave, but no one could enter. The lights went down. The first titles appeared. The audience went berserk, and then the film took over. "The applause was enormous, and when the lights came on everyone stood up but most of them didn't move," Irene Selznick remembered. "It was as though something wonderful or terrible had happened. Half an hour later there were still people standing outside. . . ." The reply cards that had been passed out were full of responses like "the greatest picture ever made," and there were no complaints about the book not having been followed exactly. The one omission the audience seemed to mind was that of Rhett Butler's "damn" at the end: Selznick would have to have one more battle with the censors.

```
AAF13 13 NT
          TDS CULVERCITY CALIF DEC 11 1939
MISS KATHARINE BROWN
GEORGIAN TERRACE HOTEL
ATLANTA GEORGIA
HAVE JUST FINISHED GONE WITH THE WIND.  GOD BLESS US ONE AND ALL.
     DAVID
```

LEFT: A relieved Selznick informs Kay Brown—already in Atlanta for première preparations—that editing is complete, scarcely a day before the press preview.

The next five weeks saw Selznick, Kern, and Fleming back in the projection room for hour after hour of piecemeal work, reducing the film in snippets and losing only one sequence in the process. Selznick invited Margaret Mitchell to come to Hollywood and see the uncut version, but she felt she wouldn't be able to keep it a secret from the inevitable reporters and curious friends. Victor Fleming, when he wasn't editing, spent September and part of October filming the additional scenes and retakes needed, including the fourth and final take of the opening porch scene, on October 13. Vivien Leigh, fresh from a vacation, looked like the sixteen-year-old Scarlett again, this time wearing the right (white) dress.

There were other obstacles to hurdle. The composer Max Steiner, who had been hired on August 14 (four months before the movie was to premiere) to write the musical score, was still not finished, and Selznick was characteristically trying to interfere with what little music Steiner had written. "I should appreciate it if you would adapt the score to use . . . the great music of the world, and of the South in particular," he wired the composer. On October 11, Selznick was still trying to coerce a very ill Ben Hecht into finishing the narrative titles for the start of the picture: "If you cannot do them immediately I will have to do them myself, which would break my heart as I have been counting, as you know, on your doing these titles. . . . Can't you swallow a bottle of thyroid and a couple of Benzedrines?" "Can do nothing but crawl in and out of bed," Hecht wired back, "tried hard to finish." Somehow the titles *were* finished, and by the middle of October the running time was under four hours.

The next preview took place on October 18, 1939,

at the Arlington Theater in Santa Barbara. As insurance against scoops, the manager was told he was going to be previewing *Intermezzo*, and the doors were locked. It was pandemonium all over again.

Ten days of shooting followed to fill in more gaps and weak spots, and Jack Cosgrove continued working on his never-ending list of special effects. He combined paintings with film, adding backgrounds, sky, clouds, rainbows, and smoke wisps, and filled in unfinished sets. His work load was so heavy that mistakes and unfinished segments started to slip by. In a panic Selznick ordered him off *Rebecca* and *Intermezzo*: He was replaceable on those. "I don't want Cosgrove to have one single thing to do between now and the time he finishes *GWTW* except *GWTW*," Selznick insisted. "A single hour taken away from finishing *GWTW* might mean thousands of dollars in revenue."

He was likewise afraid of the cost of diminishing the impact of Rhett Butler's parting shot to Scarlett O'Hara. In mid-October he took on the Hays Office, writing that "the punch line of *GWTW* . . . which forever establishes the future relationship between Scarlett and Rhett is 'Frankly, my dear, I don't give a damn.' This line is remembered, loved, and looked forward to by millions. . . . A great deal of the force and drama is dependent upon that word. . . . This word as used in the picture is not an oath or a curse, but a vulgarism, and it is so described in the Oxford English Dictionary. . . ." Selznick also asked Jock Whitney for help, suggesting, "If necessary, I think we could get the governor of Georgia and the senators and everybody else to scare Hays by saying that it was outrageous for him to consider anything so innocuous out of their Bible, a book worshiped in each of their homes, as something unfit for the scene. But I think this should be a last resort." It wasn't necessary. With other industry heavyweights, such as Hal Roach and Nick Schenck, coming to Selznick's assistance, the word was permitted, at the face-saving cost of a $5,000 fine for violating the code.

With only a month to go before the première in Atlanta, *Gone With the Wind* was still full of loose ends. Jack Cosgrove was preparing to go down with the ship in his losing battle to finish the hundreds of process shots. Max Steiner was still at work on the score (fortunately without much heed to Selznick's suggestions), and Hal Kern was still editing twenty hours a day. Entrances and exits were trimmed, all footage that was not specifically from the book was excised, and final scenes were inserted. On November 11, the very last scene, the Gettysburg List, was filmed with the Confederate bandleader, his wife, and the crying flute player (Tommy Kelly), and the technicians spliced it in. The picture was whittled down to its final length of 222 minutes; there was nothing left to cut.

To meet the demands of the publicity surrounding the pending première, a set of 145 of Walter Plunkett's costume sketches, annotated with passages from Mitchell's book, were sent to the Georgian Terrace Hotel in Atlanta. One of Scarlett's costumes and the uniform Ashley wore to Scarlett's first wedding ceremony were sent to the Atlanta Cyclorama at the personal request of Atlanta's mayor. Plunkett and Selznick, meanwhile, worked on the possibilities for promoting the movie's wardrobe, hoping for commercial tie-ins. Newspapers carried elaborate descriptions of the gowns Plunkett had designed for Vivien Leigh to wear to the première, and what Margaret Mitchell (who had lost any vestiges of her privacy in the preceding few months) would be wearing as well.

One of the most critical publicity events was to be the press preview, scheduled for December 12, at Hollywood's Four Star Theater. With 750 members, the local and national Hollywood press corps had the power to make or break Selznick's film, reporting to their huge audiences of avid movie fans. *Gone With the Wind* had been prime gossip column material for three years. But while a huge publicity buildup might find the lay public enthusiastic, the press might be vicious—feeling that it had been flimflammed by Selznick along with the bumpkins at home. For the past year Selznick had been promising the press that all would see it at the same time and that no scoops would be allowed. But one well-known columnist and radio announcer, Jimmie Fidler, tried to corner Selznick into a personal preview anyway. Fidler seemed to have a chip on his shoulder ("Spending $2 million on a movie is folly," he said in one column), but Selznick ignored the power play. With Selznick and Fleming in the audience, the preview went as planned. Any anticipated press resistance melted: As had happened in Riverside and Santa Barbara, the crowd went wild.

Almost 500,000 feet of film had been shot, 160,000 feet of which had been printed, yielding almost 29½ hours of footage. Only by editing continuously throughout filming could SIP get the film down to a tight 20,000 feet. Perhaps only by spending, at final cost, $4,230,000 could it have borne the unmistakable mark of a masterpiece. Part god, part puppeteer, David O. Selznick had done the impossible against tremendous odds. He had prepared a colossal motion picture in four months: It should have taken him at least a year.

Selznick International Pictures

cordially invites you to the
initial press showing of

Margaret Mitchell's

"Gone with the Wind"

Starring Clark Gable, Vivien Leigh, Leslie Howard and Olivia deHavilland

Screen play by Sidney Howard   Directed by Victor Fleming

Produced by David O. Selznick

A Selznick International Picture, Released by Loew's, Inc.

at the Four Star Theatre

on Tuesday, December the twelfth
nineteen hundred and thirty-nine
promptly at two o'clock
in the afternoon.

(This showing is exclusively for members of the press)

"Gone With The Wind"
Preview Questionnaire

THE PRODUCERS WILL BE GRATEFUL FOR ANSWERS TO EACH OF THE QUESTIONS BELOW. *IF MAILED WITHIN TWENTY-FOUR HOURS* THEY WILL BE HAPPY TO SEND A PHOTOGRAPH OF ONE OF THE FOLLOWING:

PLEASE) ☐ Clark Gable
CHECK) ☐ Vivien Leigh
ONE) ☐ Leslie Howard
ONLY) ☐ Olivia De Havilland

1. How did you like the picture? *The most wonderful, interesting and breath taking picture I've ever witnessed. I never enjoyed anything as such.*

2. Was the action of the picture entirely clear? If not, where was it confusing? *How could Scarlet O'Hara, start up, building up cotton fields, the home + etc, with nothing to start. 1 pr. gold earrings in jewel box + that the father held as keepsake + soldier tried to steal would bring nothing. everything was gone ———.*

3. Was the sound entirely clear and could you understand the dialogue? If not, do you recall which parts were not audible? *Yes, with exception of a few remarks of a colored worker.*

4. Did any parts seem too long? If so, what parts? *Yes, the kissing of Ret Butler + wife too long + suggestive for young folks to witness.*

5. What did you think of the cast? *Splendid, especially the colored mammy marvelous + natural.*

6. Have you any other suggestions to make? *Why make such an issue of all the dead bodies + so long a procedure. The escape of R + Butler in wagon as town burns at his heels is slap stick comedy. to far fetched for rest of picture.*

7. Do you think the picture should be played with an intermission? *Yes. Unless 1 hr of film is cut it needs intermission as to give one time to think.*

8. Will you come to see the picture again? *Yes*

9. What, for you, would be the most convenient time of day to start the picture, both for matinee and evening performances? In answering this question, please bear in mind that the picture with an intermission will be four hours long.
1.30 p.m. + 8. oclock prompt p.m.

10. Do you think the picture should be played with continuous performances all day, or only at specified times as is the case with a play? *as a play, as there is so much to it.*

11. Would you prefer to buy reserved seats? *yes, if twice a day performance*

12. What scale of admission prices do you think should be charged? And would you be prepared to pay a higher price if the producers went to the expense of having only two or three shows a day, with reserved seats? *75¢*

Name *Henry's*

Address *815½ State St*   City *Santa Barbara Calf.*

LEFT: A still hard-working Vivien Leigh poses for a publicity photo of a dress Walter Plunkett created for her to wear at the Junior League costume ball, in the style of the other dresses she wore in GWTW: black Lyons velvet trimmed with ermine, with a matching ermine cape. Selznick later gave the dress to the actress as a gift.

OPPOSITE: Leigh poses in the gold lamé gown Plunkett designed for her appearance at the Atlanta première: gold-sequined, rose-quilted sleeves and a 22" waist.

PRECEDING PAGES, LEFT: Invitation to the December 12 press preview, including very abbreviated credits.

PRECEDING PAGES, RIGHT: Questionnaire from the Santa Barbara preview on October 18, 1939. Selznick was near frantic about the previews and sent his publicity staff a barrage of telegrams. In 1974, Howard Dietz recalled, "As MGM had invested Clark Gable and [$1.25] million in this . . . picture, and as I represented MGM in promoting it, the marketing with all its complications was in my care. David O. Selznick, brilliant producer though he was, was also in my care, in a sense. His fixation was telegrams. Not a day went by when he didn't send me a yard or two from California. They usually arrived in the dead of night and, living in a New York town house with several stories, as I did, I found it especially annoying to be summoned to the door at an ungodly hour. One Selznick telegram totaled a record 4 feet high. . . . I was ashamed to let the servants see the size of this extravagant memo that woke them up. It read in part: 'I want you to be very careful of the paper you select for the program STOP Sometimes their crackling makes it difficult to hear the dialogue STOP Promise you will attend to this.' I telegraphed back: 'Received your epigram STOP You can rest assured about the program noise STOP However have made tie-up with Gone With the Wind Peanut Brittle Company assuring each patron of the picture a box of peanut brittle as he enters the theater.' "

CHAPTER NINE
The Atlanta Première

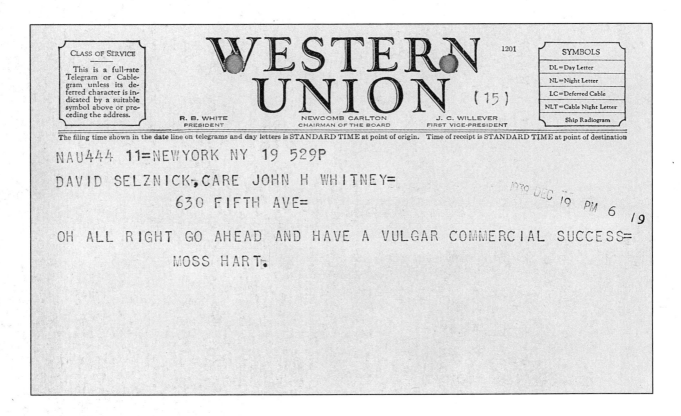

ABOVE: *Dramatist Moss Hart's telegram of mock resignation to Selznick following the success of the Atlanta première.*

OPPOSITE: *Los Angeles, 12:40 A.M. on Wednesday, December 13. Laurence Olivier, Irene Selznick, Olivia de Havilland, David Selznick, and Vivien Leigh board the DC-3 bound for Atlanta. De Havilland went despite being forbidden to by Warner Brothers' boss, Jack Warner.*

Credits

The authors wish to thank:

Olivia de Havilland, George Cukor, Wilbur G. Kurtz, Jr., Franklin Garrett, Jim Jackson, Nina Burnham Jackson, Ted Turner, Yvette Curran, Robert Cushman, Prentiss L. Moore, Laurie S. Christman, Dr. Ilona R. Hirsch, Robert E. Weiss, Anne Dodds, Barbara Schlain, Dr. Raymond Daum, Anne Salter, Lucia Robinson Wayne, Larry Gulley, Joyce Jelks, Florence A. Koenig, Georgia Rawley, Decherd Turner, Patrick Keeley, Marc Wanamaker, Mary Hall Mayer, Jodi Goldstein, Pat Arnold, Peter Bateman, Barbara Berner, Mildred Branch, Herb Bridges, Charlesey and Eugene Brown, Carolyn Busby, Sonya Z. Cohen, Florence Connell, Mary Corliss, Rose and John Cunningham, Devereux Danna, Henry Diltz, Jeanne Drewsen, Kenneth Fay, Robert Gable, Yves Ginoux, Keith Glaser, Jim Greer, Dwight L. Grell, Frances Harwood, Ronald Haver, Mike Hawks, Margaret Herrick, Allan Herzer, Lance Holden, Richard Hudson, Inada Photo Lab, Deborah James, Kathy Kettlew, Claudia Kunze, Elma Kurtz, Fred Latasa, Kathleen MacLennon, Anne Mahony, Craig Maurer, Donna, Marty and Melly Meadows, Angus McBean, Frances Milburg, Lisa Mitchell, Walter O'Connor, Edmund F. Petersen, Darlene Parrish, Michele Purdy, Jack Rabin, William Reilly, Kiawii Russell, Richard B. Skolnick, Leonore and Paul Smith, John Taylor, David and Matthew Thomson, Philip Tripoli, Craig Williams, Ralph B. Young, Dave Zimmer • GWTW: Margaret Baugh, Rand Brooks, Fred Crane, Cammie King, Vivien Leigh, Sunny Alexander Lash, Stephens Mitchell, Carroll Nye, Fred Parrish, Joseph B. Platt, Marcella Rabwin, Lyle Wheeler • THE DAVID O. SELZNICK COLLECTION: Harry Ranson Humanities Research Center; The University of Texas, Austin, Texas, Thomas Staley, director; Dr. Charles Bell, Dr. W. H. Crain, Paul M. Bailey, Sarah Capps, Ricardo Castillo, Diana Jones, Mary Mallory, Michelle Patterson, Anna Vitek, Alison von Eberstein, Steven Yount • TURNER ENTERTAINMENT COMPANY: Alison Hill, Roger Mayer, Jack Petrick, Richard P. May, Kathy Manolis • NEW YORK PUBLIC LIBRARY: Rare Books and Manuscripts, Robert Sink • HARVARD UNIVERSITY, HARVARD THEATRE COLLECTION: Dr. Jeanne Newlin, Catherine Johnson • EMORY UNIVERSITY, ATLANTA, GEORGIA, ROBERT WOODRUFF LIBRARY: Dr. Linda Matthews, Beverly D. Bishop, Ellen Nemhauser, Elizabeth K. Knox • THE UNIVERSITY OF GEORGIA: Thomas E. Camden • ATLANTA HISTORICAL SOCIETY: John Ott, president; Elaine Kirkland; William A. Richards; Nancy White; Ted Ryan • ATLANTA-FULTON PUBLIC LIBRARY: Ronald A. Dubberly, director; Casper Jordan; Janice Sikes; Sarah Alexander • KOBAL COLLECTION: Simon Crocker, David Kent, Christine Lloyd-Lyons (London), Robert Cosenza (New York).

TWELFTH ANNUAL AWARDS PRESE[NT]
ACADEMY OF MOTION PICTURE AR[TS]

COCOANUT GROVE AMBASSADOR H[OTEL]
FEBRUARY 29, 1940

RIGHT: David O. Selznick and Vivien Leigh in the lobby of the Ambassador Hotel after being nearly mobbed by fans outside. As they entered the hotel, they received the biggest ovation of the night.
OPPOSITE: The menu.

OVERLEAF, LEFT: Vivien Leigh in a quiet moment with her award.
OVERLEAF, RIGHT: After the Academy Awards, Victor Fleming holds his Oscar for Best Director. Selznick had accepted it for the absent Fleming, from the director Mervyn LeRoy.

Even before the list of nominations for the twelfth annual Academy Awards was released on February 12, 1940, speculation on the nominees was running high. Various press types and movie industry denizens were miffed that David O. Selznick had slipped *Gone With the Wind* into the contest at the last minute, as 1939 was already being touted as the best year yet, with a plethora of exceptionally fine pictures already released. It must have appeared to some that Selznick was gilding the lily by throwing his epic blockbuster into the ring so late. But actually, Selznick, with his penchant for literary sources and high production standards, should be credited with the increase in quality films at the end of the 1930s, as other studios tried to meet the new standards of the art.

It seemed that all the stars had been busy that year. George Cukor had directed *The Women* with five rejected Scarlett candidates; Gable had also appeared in *Idiot's Delight*, and Leslie Howard accompanied Ingrid Bergman in her debut in *Intermezzo*. Carole Lombard was featured in two films, *In Name Only* with Cary Grant, and *Made for Each Other* with Jimmy Stewart, which was also produced by David Selznick. There was even some good original screenwriting, as *Mr. Smith Goes to Washington* attests. Legendary screen goddesses Greta Garbo and Marlene Dietrich revealed their comedic talents, in *Ninotchka* and *Destry Rides Again*, respectively. Motion pictures running the gamut from Westerns to a Shirley Temple feature were represented in this touchstone year. *Gone With the Wind* had a lot of excellent competition.

GWTW earned a record thirteen nominations in twelve categories (de Havilland and McDaniel were both named for Best Supporting Actress, and McDaniel's inclusion broke the color barrier). When awards day, February 29, 1940, arrived, the results of the balloting were still secret, but, as was customary, the newspapers had been given the list of winners to publish after the ceremony. In the fervor of that year the *Los Angeles Times* couldn't resist and splashed its afternoon edition with giant headlines: David O. Selznick was going to do to the Academy Awards what General William T. Sherman had done to

The Los Angeles Ambassador
LOS ANGELES, CALIFORNIA

Suggestion Menu for

Mr. __Academy of Motion Picture Arts & Sciences__ Party

Address_____ Phone_____

Number in Party_____

Date and Time __February 29, 1940.__

Room __Cocoanut Grove__

Canape of Fresh Lobster, Georgette

Hearts of Celery   Ripe Jumbo Olives

Essence of Tomato Madrilene en Tasse

Grilled Filet Mignon, Maitre d'Hotel

or

Breast of Capon Saute with Fresh Mushrooms and Virginia Ham,
Colbert

Parisian Potatoes   Fresh String Beans, Julienne

Endive and Grapefruit, Lemon Dressing

Individual Bombe Glace, Melba   Petits Fours

Demi Tasse

EXTRAS

Cigars_____

Cigarettes_____   Menu Prepared by_____

Flowers_____   _____

Favors_____

Music_____   Maitre d'Hotel_____

FORM 501

"Fay Bainter" and Myself—at Academy "Award Dinner" Feb. 29.'40

Georgia. Thus began the Academy's famous system of sealed envelopes.

Clark Gable knew he had not won Best Actor, but came anyway with Carole Lombard. It was his third nomination, and he had already won an Oscar. Thomas Mitchell won Best Supporting Actor, but for *Stagecoach*, although his role in *GWTW* may have helped. Vivien Leigh was in a tough race for Best Actress against Greer Garson in *Goodbye, Mr. Chips*, Bette Davis in *Dark Victory*, Irene Dunne in *Love Affair*, and Greta Garbo in *Ninotchka*. But her sweet victory was not the slightest bit controversial. Her acceptance speech focused on "... that composite figure of energy, courage, and very great kindness, in whom all points of *GWTW* meet, Mr. David Selznick." But by far the loudest ovation of the evening went to Hattie McDaniel, who won the first Oscar ever awarded to a black performer. It would also be the last one for twenty-four years.

When Selznick came to the podium to accept the Oscar for Best Picture, he knew he had beaten the best. The other nominees were *Dark Victory; Goodbye, Mr. Chips; Love Affair; Mr. Smith Goes to Washington; Ninotchka; Of Mice and Men; Stagecoach; The Wizard of Oz;* and *Wuthering Heights*—a veritable pantheon of screen classics. He was also awarded the Irving G. Thalberg Award for "consistent excellent of production" —not an award specifically for *GWTW*, but Selznick's publicity people would claim it as such.

Victor Fleming was named Best Director, Sidney Howard was named for Screenplay; Hal Kern and James Newcom shared the award for Film Editing; Ernest Haller and Ray Rennahan shared the Oscar for Cinematography; and Lyle Wheeler won for Art Direction. William Cameron Menzies wrapped up the *GWTW* sweep with a special award for "outstanding achievement in the use of color for the enhancement of dramatic mood in the production of *GWTW*." About the only deserving participants in *GWTW* who went unrewarded were Max Steiner who lost the award for Music (Original Score) to Herbert Stothart (*The Wizard of Oz*), Jack Cosgrove for Special Effects, and Walter Plunkett, who received no recognition for his superlative costuming. Academy recognition for costume design was still nine years away.

GWTW had won a record-breaking eight Oscars, ten counting Menzies' award and the Thalberg Award. Selznick's sweep was so thorough that it prompted emcee Bob Hope to quip: "Really, I think this is a wonderful thing, a benefit like this for David Selznick."

ABOVE: David Selznick, Vivien Leigh, Olivia de Havilland, and John Hay Whitney stop for photographers on their way into the Cocoanut Grove. "The war in Europe and plans for our future were all secondary to Academy Awards night, which was looming, a topic we superstitiously avoided," recalled Irene Selznick. "Despite many nominations, David had never won an Oscar. He had promised me one 'someday.' This year was surely it.

"The build-up to that night was tremendous. We had several tables in the Cocoanut Grove; our guests were the GWTW nominees and those who accompanied them. Everyone met at our house for drinks. When it was time to leave, we spread out in the courtyard. In a flash I saw David get into the first limousine with Clark and Vivien and their escorts and drive away, with nary a look behind. I'd been forgotten."

ABOVE: Douglas Fairbanks, Jr., Laurence Olivier, and Vivien Leigh at the dinner table. RIGHT: Fay Bainter, Spencer Tracy, and Vivien Leigh, who would leave her Oscar with friend and secretary Sonny Alexander after returning to England with Olivier during the war. Tracy, 1938's Best Actor, presented 1939's Oscar to Leigh. Victor Fleming had been largely responsible for the hard-edged persona of Clark Gable, while it was the perceptive George Cukor who had helped Leigh. "As a result of Gone With the Wind, she was the hottest thing in pictures, she was an established, big movie star," said Cukor. "In all this, her professional attitude toward Larry [Olivier] never changed in the slightest. . . . He was the great, talented actor, and she a promising young, not-too-important actress who had not yet accomplished a great deal. Her success as a picture actress never seemed to matter to her. She wanted to accomplish things on Larry's terms."

OVERLEAF: Selznick receives the Irving G. Thalberg Memorial Award from Dr. Ernest Martin Hopkins, president of Dartmouth College, Thalberg's alma mater, "for the most consistent high quality of production in 1939."

Selznick recalled, ". . . In fact, it was I who suggested the Thalberg Memorial Award, in an attempt to perpetuate the standards that Thalberg stood for, and as an incentive to people to try to make every film that they did just as good as they could possibly make it. . . ."

Statistics

Statistical Report of Completed Production

Title of picture: *Gone With the Wind*
Production Number 108

George Cukor—Director
Start Date: Jan. 26, 1939
Finish Date: Feb. 15, 1939

Suspension Period
Start Date: Feb. 16, 1939
Finish Date: Mar. 1, 1939

Victor Fleming—Director★
Start Date: Mar. 2, 1939
Finish Date: July 1, 1939

CAST. *Clark Gable, Vivien Leigh, Leslie Howard, Olivia de Havilland, Oscar Polk, George Reeves, Alicia Rhett, Victor Jory, Eddie Anderson, Hattie McDaniel, Thomas Mitchell, Barbara O'Neil, Ona Munson, Fred Crane, Jane Darwell, Isabel Jewell, Mickey Kuhn, Paul Hurst, Butterfly McQueen, Ann Rutherford, Evelyn Keyes, Laura Hope Crews, Harry Davenport, Rand Brooks, Everett Brown, Carroll Nye, Cammie King.*

STAFF. Directors: *Victor Fleming, Sam Wood, George Cukor;* Assistant Directors: *Eric Stacey, Reggie Callow;* Art Director: *Lyle Wheeler;* Production Design: *William Cameron Menzies;* Interior Decorations: *Joseph Platt;* Set Dressings: *Howard Bristol;* Film Editors: *Hal C. Kern, James Newcom;* Cameramen: *Ernest Haller, Ray Rennahan;* Recorder: *Frank Maher;* Script Clerks: *Lydia Schiller, Connie Earle;* 2d Unit Directors: *William*

★In collaboration with Mr. Sam Wood

Number of days of original schedule: 72 (exclusive of 2d units)
Number of days of revised schedule: 128 (exclusive of 2d units)

1st unit shooting days
Total:	125 days work, 12 days idle, 137 days total
George Cukor:	18 days of shooting (as of 7–1–39)
Victor Fleming:	93 days of shooting (as of 7–1–39)
Sam Wood:	24 days of shooting (as of 7–1–39)

(Note: Fleming and Wood worked as a single unit for 2 days. They worked as separate units simultaneously for 8 days. This explains the difference of 10 days in shooting as shown above)

Shooting days of retakes, added scenes, pickup shots, inserts, etc., following close of picture: 24 days of shooting

Number of days devoted to sound tracks, trailer, and effects following close of picture: 4 days of recording

Number of days shooting tests (at studio only): 42 Days

2d unit shooting days including retakes
Local 2d units (including 40 Acres, Studio, Lasky Mesa:	33 days of shooting
Chico 2nd unit (including 9 days idle):	22 days
Big Bear 2d unit (including 1 day idle):	6 days
Fitzpatrick 2d unit (including travel time):	20 days

Number of stills shot
4″ × 5″: 3,286
8″ × 10″: 5,435

Film footage used
Burning of Atlanta unit, 8 cameras	11,378	(including B & W)
1st Unit (Fleming-Cukor-Wood as of 7–1–39)	343,950	
1st Unit (Wood–as of 7–1–39)	28,773	
Local 2d units (as of 7–1–39)	56,973	
Big Bear unit (Eason), complete	7,299	
Chico unit (Franklin), complete	8,074	
Fitzpatrick unit, complete	4,892	
Total footage used on production as of 7–1–39		461,339
Tests (at studio only) (including B & W footage)	120,095	

Statistical Report of Completed Production *(cont.)*

Menzies, Chester Franklin, Breezy Eason, Ballbusch, Fitzpatrick; 2d Unit Assistant Directors: *Harve Foster, Ralph Slosser, John Sherwood;* 2d Unit Cameramen: *Will Cline, Ray Rennahan.*

Footage Used following Close of Picture on 7–1–39	60,463		
Total of Tests and Following Footage		180,558	
Total Footage Used (including Technicolor and B & W)			641,897
Sound footage as of close of picture (7–1–39)	417,735		
Sound footage following close of picture	70,366		
Sound footage used on tests	85,332		
Total sound footage used			573,431
Scoring and prerecording at Goldwyn Studios			
Music track footage used	182,140	182,140	
Scoring days at Goldwyn Studios	19		
Dubbing and recording at Goldwyn Studios			
Dubbing footage used	402,483	402,483	
Dubbing days at Goldwyn Studios	57		

SCREEN CREDITS FOR *GWTW.* Produced by *David O. Selznick;* Directed by *Victor Fleming;* Screenplay by *Sidney Howard;* Musical Score by *Max Steiner;* Production designed by *William Cameron Menzies;* Special Photographic Effects by *Jack Cosgrove;* Photographed by *Ernest Haller;* Technicolor Associates: *Ray Rennahan, A.S.C.,* and *Wilfrid M. Cline, A.S.C.;* Art Direction by *Lyle Wheeler;* Interiors by *Joseph Platt;* Interior Decoration by *Edward G. Boyle;* Costumes designed by *Walter Plunkett;* Supervising Film Editor: *Hal C. Kern;* Associate Film Editor: *James E. Newcom;* Scenario Assistant: *Barbara Keon.*

PROGRAM CREDITS FOR *GWTW.* Produced by *David O. Selznick;* Directed by *Victor Fleming;* Based on Margaret Mitchell's Novel, *Gone With the Wind;* Screenplay by *Sidney Howard;* The production designed by *William Cameron Menzies;* Art Direction by *Lyle Wheeler;* Photographed by *Ernest Haller, A.S.C.;* Technicolor Associates: *Ray Rennahan, A.S.C.,* and *Wilfrid M. Cline, A.S.C.;* Musical Score by *Max Steiner;* Musical Score Associate: *Lou Forbes;* Special Photographic Effects by *Jack Cosgrove;* Associate (Fire Effects): *Lee Zavitz;* Costumes Designed by *Walter Plunkett;* Scarlett's Hats by *John Frederics;* Interiors by *Joseph B. Platt;* Interior decoration by *Edward G. Boyle;* Supervising Film Editor: *Hal C. Kern;* Associate Film Editor: *James E. Newcom;* Scenario Assistant: Barbara Keon; Recorder: *Frank Maher;* Makeup and Hair Styling: *Monty Westmore;* Associates: *Hazel Rogers and Ben Nye;* Dance Directors: *Frank Floyd and Eddie Prinz;* Historian: *Wilbur G. Kurtz;* Technical Advisers: *Susan Myrick and Will Price;* Research: *Lillian K. Deighton;* Production Manager: *Raymond A. Klune;* Technicolor Co. Supervision: *Natalie Kalmus;* Associate: *Henri Jaffa;* Assistant Director: *Eric G. Stacey;* Second Assistant Director: *Ridgeway Callow;* Production Continuity: *Lydia Schiller and Connie Earle;* Mechanical Engineer: *R.D. Musgrave;* Construction Superintendant: *Harold Fenton;* Chief Grip: *Fred Williams;* In Charge of Wardrobe: *Edward P. Lambert;* Associates: *Marion Dabney and Elmer Ellsworth;* Casting Managers: *Charles Richards and Fred Schuessler;* Location Manager: *Mason Litson;* Scenic Department Superintendant: *Henry J. Stahl;* Electrical Superintendant: *Wally Oettel;* Chief Electrician: *James Potevin;* Properties Manager: *Harold Coles;* On the Set: *Arden Cripe;* Greens: *Roy A. McLaughlin;* Drapes: *James Forney;* Special properties made by *Ross B. Jackson;* Tara Landscaped by *Florence Yoch;* Still photographer: *Fred Parrish;*

Camera operators: *Arthur Arling and Vincent Farrar;* Assistant Film Editors: *Richard van Enger and Ernest Leadley.*

GWTW STAFF LIST (CREW). Director: *George Cukor;* Assistant Director: *Eric Stacey;* Second Assistant Director: *Reggie Callow;* Production Manager: *Ray Klune;* Production Assistant: *Will McCune;* Location Manager: *Mason Litson;* Continuity: *Barbara Keon;* Script Clerk: *Connie Earle;* Script Clerk: *Lydia Schiller;* Art Department: *William Menzies;* Art Department: *Lyle Wheeler;* Cast Director: *Charles Richards;* Assistant Cast Director: *Harvey Clermont;* Set Dresser: *Eddie Boyle;* Prop Manager: *Harold Coles;* Company Prop Man: *Arden Cripe;* 2d Prop Man: *George Rule;* Green Man: *Roy McLaughlin;* Camera Department: *Roy Overbaugh;* 1st Cameraman: *Lee Garmes;* Technical Cameraman: *Will Cline;* 2d Cameraman: *Roy Clark;* Assistant Cameraman: *Paul Hill;* Still Man: *Fred Parrish;* Company Grip: *Fred Williams;* Gaffer: *James Potevin;* Rigger: *R. B. Campbell;* Electrical Department head: *Wally Oettel;* Mixer: *Frank Maher;* Makeup Head: *Monty Westmore;* Makeup Assistant: *Ben Nye;* Hairdress Head: *Hazel Rogers;* Wardrobe Head: *Edward Lambert;* Men's Wardrobe: *Elmer Ellsworth;* Women's Wardrobe: *Marion Dabney;* Film Editor: *Hal Kern;* Construction: *Harold Fenton;* Purchasing and Transportation: *George Doan and Joyce Allen;* Camera Effects: *Jack Cosgrove;* Research: *Wilbur Kurtz;* Research: *Susan Myrick;* Special Effects: *Lee Zavitz;* Process: *Don Musgrave.*

ACADEMY AWARDS. Nominations announced: Monday, February 12, 1940; Awards presented: Thursday, Febraury 29, 1940, at the Cocoanut Grove of the Los Angeles Ambassador Hotel; Banquet—Bob Hope MC for last half only.
NOMINATIONS AND AWARDS. Picture★ accepted by David O Selznick (presented by Y. Frank Freeman); Actor: Clark Gable as "Rhett Butler"; Actress: *Vivien Leigh*★ as "Scarlett O'Hara" (presented by Spencer Tracy); Supporting Actress: Olivia de Havilland as "Melanie Hamilton;" and *Hattie McDaniel*★ as "Mammy" (presented by Fay Bainter); Art Direction: *Lyle Wheeler*★ (presented by Darryl F. Zannuck); Cinematography (color): *Ernest Haller*★, *Ray Rennahan*★ (presented by Darryl F. Zanuck); Directing: Victor Fleming★ accepted by David O. Selznick (presented by Mervyn LeRoy); Film Editing: *Hal C. Kern*★, *James Newcom*★ (presented by Darryl F. Zanuck); Musical (original score): Max Steiner; Sound Recording: Samuel Goldwyn Studio Department—Thomas T. Moulton, Sound Director; Special Effects: John R. Cosgrove, Frank Albin, Arthur Johns (Special Technical Award nomination); Writing (Screenplay): Sidney Howard★ post humous award; no acceptor noted (presented by Sinclair Lewis); Scientific or Technical Awards (Class III)†: Multiple award for important contributions in cooperative development of new improved process projection equipment to F. R. Abbott, Haller Belt, Alan Cook and Bausch & Lomb Optical Co. for faster projection lenses, to Mitchell Camera Co. for a new type of process projection lenses, to Mitchell Camera Co. for a new type of process projection head, to Mole-Richardson Co. for a new type of automatically controlled projection arc lamp, to Charles Handley, David Joy, and National Carbon Corp. for improved and more stable high-intensity carbons, to Winton Hoch and Technicolor Motion Picture Corp. for an auxilliary optical system, to Don Musgrave and Selznick International Pictures, Inc., for pioneering in the use of coordinated equipment in the production of *Gone With the Wind* plaque (presented by Darryl F. Zanuck); Irving G. Thalberg Memorial award†: to *David O. Selznick* (presented by Dr. Ernest Martin Hopkins, President of Dartmouth University, location of the Thalberg Memorial Library).

★Denotes winner
†Award not in competition; does not count as a nomination.
††Award not in competition; does not count as a nomination; not to be counted with picture.
Note: Acceptor(s) are in italics, unless otherwise noted.

Index

OPPOSITE: *Atlanta, 1961. Vivien Leigh, Olivia de Havilland, and David O. Selznick help Atlanta relive the festivities of the original 1939 première. Gable had just passed away. In the rear to the left, looking down toward the stars, is Selznick's son Daniel.*